FLIP

THE PYRAMID

Contents

To my beautiful wife Kirsten, our two awesome children, Anneliese and Dashiell, and our loving Bernese Mountain Dog, Chili.

Acknowledgments

This book was truly a tribal journey, and there are many people to thank.

We first began in the summer of 2010, when we assembled a voluntary team of Ambrosians to create a presentation reflective of what we had learned, and what had transformed Ambrose, over the previous three years. We called this our "summer project" and we had a lot of fun working together. I sincerely thank the team members: Brian Bichler, Maya Cohen, Marc Dwek, Marisa Gomes, Alex Koykova, Kelly Lee, Julie Murray, Josh Newman and Jack Speece. We brought a lot of enthusiasm and passion to this project, and I have since given this presentation internally to every new employee and externally to well over 100 groups around the country.

I love giving this presentation and am invigorated at every event. I owe a huge thank you to David Ades, who has been the lead in arranging my speaking opportunities, and who has an unbelievable ability to find great audiences. Of course, I also have to extend great thanks to my friend, Coach Leonard Peters, who helped get my speaking skills to a whole new level.

In January 2011 I began blogging about this journey—a pursuit that essentially yielded the first rough draft of this book. Stacey Molski was invaluable to the process. She vetted every blog post. Her insights and suggestions were excellent. I also want to thank everyone who read and sent me comments, either publicly or in email, as their feedback provided me with early, helpful guidance.

Ambrose's business coach, Coach Roger Merriam, also has been instrumental in helping us transform Ambrose and moving us to a much better place. We could not have done it without Roger.

I must also thank Eric Foodim, Hugh LaRoche, Marc Dwek and, the entire 'Brose Nation for enthusiastically embracing this new way, reading so many of the books I recommended, and finding other books, and helping make Ambrose a much happier Nation.

A huge thank you also is due to each of my fellow Ambrosians who shared in this book their perspective on this wonderful journey: Annie Abbondante, Ariel Merkrebs-Finkelstein, Christopher Gaine, Christine Pesaturo, Dave Zodikoff, Hugh LaRoche, Jacqui Brady, Jim Andrews, John Devivo, Josh Newman, Kim Diorio, Kyle Grubman, Lee Schatzberg, Maribel Morales, Marvelle Roberts, Matt Thomas, Stacey Molski, Maya Cohen and Steven Caldwell. All are true compatriots in this great journey of ours.

Finally, Michael Roney, my editor and publisher, has been a true professional to work with on making this book happen. He has made the processes enjoyable. Thank you, Michael.

Introduction

How to Unleash Your Success Story

Individual heroics, brute force, micromanagement, command and control. These things will get you only so far in managing the workforce of a growing organization. This sort of journey is hard, miserable and unpleasant. I travelled that road for 12 years after the launch of my company. It was a slog, and I became very unhappy with my "job" as an entrepreneur. I wanted to quit! We got to about 35 employees, and we were relatively successful, but we were stuck in the mud and exhausted. We had reached the end of that road and just weren't going any farther.

I knew there had to be a better way to manage the growth of our human capital, so I embarked on an intense learning journey. I read more than 100 business books, some excellent, some not. I attended dozens of business seminars, and devoured each issue of the *Harvard Business Review*. I got others around me to start doing the same, and we saw a much, much different way. The first several years of this process were hard, but then things got dramatically better.

Once we found this very different way, a way in which all of the people in our company were aligned, empowered and engaged, we began to rock and roll. We began to grow with aplomb, and our growth and profits accelerated. Our journey became much more enjoyable, and we started going to better places. I wish I had figured this all out much earlier in life.

A fully actualized workforce is an exciting thing to behold. What follows in these pages is what we have learned and what we have done to implement this much better, easier journey to success.

ON FIRE: LIBERATING YOUR MOST VALUABLE ASSET

To be successful—all you can be—your organization's leadership must learn that human capital is its most important asset. Your leaders then must structure and arrange the organization's environment to enable individuals to thrive—to get the best out of everyone. Building an environment that helps everyone to participate, contribute and achieve must become a strategic imperative.

If every organization were to do this, our economy and society would be in a much better place. People working in an aligned, engaged and empowered way tend to feel great about themselves—they get to the top of Maslow's "hierarchy of needs" (self-actualization), which in turn allows them and their companies to achieve big things.

You can move mountains when this is done in the right way. What's more, doing so is your obligation to the organization and its people.

Unfortunately, most organizational leaders do not understand this imperative. Or, if they do, they have no darn idea how to deliver on it. For years, I was in that category, but I continued to read, study, listen and experiment. I found an incredible amount of literature on this topic, as well as many others who have successfully gone down this road. No need for a lot of original thinking. This road is rather well marked; you just need to find it.

It will take time, however. *Results will not be immediate.* There will be naysayers—people who want to hold fast to the well-known "command and control" approach to leadership.

WHERE I WANT TO TAKE YOU

I have two primary goals for this book. The first is to help you realize the importance of this mindset shift toward your organization's human capital. Professor Douglas McGregor wrote about this mindset shift in his 1960 book, *The Human Side of Enterprise*, in which he articulated his Theory X and Theory Y. Theory X assumes people are lazy, will shirk work, and therefore need to be micromanaged through command and control. Theory Y, in stark contrast, assumes that people are ambitious and self-motivated, take pride and satisfaction in their work and their achievements, but need the proper organizational environment to bring this human attribute to fruition.

Based on 16 years in business, I am a firm believer in McGregor's Theory Y. I hope this book makes you a believer as well. This mindset shift is a necessary prerequisite for unleashing your organization's human capital.

My second goal in writing this book is to give you a proven methodology to execute on McGregor's Theory Y. Please note, however, that a *sine qua non* is leadership's abandonment of Theory X (command and control) and embracement of Theory Y (aligned liberation). That first step, letting go, isn't easy for many people, but it is a mandatory requirement. Once you make that pivot in your mindset, you then can rely on the seven necessary organizational components to execute on Theory Y, all of which I explain in detail in these pages.

These seven components for success are as follows:

1. A Constitutional Framework

2. A disciplined meeting rhythm

3. Metrics literacy

4. A tribal culture

5. An obsession with communicating

6. Embracement of change, risk and failure

7. Great people and physical and mental wellness

Within this organizational construct, you'll be able to let go, liberate your human capital and achieve big things.

BUILDING YOUR CONSTITUTIONAL FRAMEWORK

To play a great game, people need to know its rules, purpose and goals. How can you step back and let your people take the field and play their best unless they know that stuff? If you simply stop micromanaging, if you simply dispense with command and control, you will run astray.

When this occurs, the unfortunate knee-jerk reaction is to revert to micromanagement and say "Look what happens! People need to be micromanaged!" This is the wrong, emotional response—Professor McGregor's Theory X. I tried that and it doesn't work.

On the contrary, you need to build a *Constitutional Framework*, the organizational construct that sets the rules and the goals that enable people to play an excellent game—allowing them to self-actualize. This concept is central to this book, and so important that I capitalize it. You need to put an incredible amount of time, energy, thought and faith into building the environment and the organizational construct that will provide guidance and support self-actualization in an aligned, engaged and empowered manner.

So how do you build your Constitutional Framework? The details are in the subsequent chapters, but I'll tell you right now that you need to begin with core values, a core purpose, a brand promise and objectively measurable goals. This is classic Jim Collins (more about him later). This framework, if strong and vivid, provides every individual in your organization with the guidance they need to self-actualize—to take tactical action steps with confidence, within clearly defined behavioral boundaries and toward clearly defined goals. Everything else flows from there.

A TRIBAL CULTURE

Once you have that Constitutional Framework, you can nourish a powerful tribal culture. Many founders, entrepreneurs and leaders just don't get this: We are tribal animals. We are pack animals.

Too many leaders are too focused on their own egos. They think it is all about them. It isn't. Leaders must shift their focus to everyone else. You have to deliver an awesome tribal experience to everyone in your company. This is a responsibility of leadership. People want, *people crave*, a tribal experience. It is human nature. It is simple. People want to belong to something bigger, to something exciting, to a movement, to a journey. So leadership must deliver this experience.

This is why we join civic organizations, political movements, religious organizations, clubs, follow sports teams, but with no real need to understand why. Just understand that we like to belong to something bigger than ourselves. So give this to people. And let them take an ownership interest in your organization's culture. This is an essential element to building an aligned, engaged and empowered workforce. People will thank you for this.

A strong, healthy, positive culture is also one of your most important assets. It protects all stakeholders: employees, family members, partners, shareholders, lenders, vendors, clients, the community and our government. Is your culture healthy enough? Is it strong enough? Leadership must constantly worry about the organization's tribal culture.

OUR BACK-STORY: HOW WE LEARNED WHAT WE LEARNED

My own company's Constitutional Framework and tribal culture has proven to be powerfully effective, and it's getting better every day. However, it didn't happen overnight. It also wasn't created in a vacuum or solely through theoretical discussions in a conference room. Instead, it was born from experience—the fits and starts we had as a rapidly growing company in the late 1990s and early 2000s. What we experienced in those often heady and sometimes frustrating days informed our unique path to the realizations that have resulted in what we call our *Flip the Pyramid* approach.

Because our own experience as a startup was central to the success we're enjoying now, I've included our back-story in this book's first two chapters. As you read them, I hope that they resonate in ways that provide additional perspective on your own issues and aspirations as you prepare for your journey toward becoming a fully functioning, aligned and self-actualized organization. At that point, you will be fully prepped and equipped for the main course—the blueprint for success encompassed by Part Two.

ACHIEVING BIG THINGS

The responsibility of an organization's leadership is setting people up for success in their job and in life, enabling them to feel great about what they are doing every single day—and to do it in an aligned way where everyone is individually and collectively moving toward clearly defined goals. This requires a full-time commitment on the part of leadership and the organization. Again, it isn't easy, but it is absolutely achievable.

I truly hope you enjoy this book and are successful in putting these methodologies into practice. With your full commitment to the principles and practices described in this book, I'm confident that everyone in your organization, including you, will ultimately love what you are doing, and will achieve big things. I look forward to hearing about your success.

Oh…and don't forget to have fun on the journey.

Part One

1

From Concept
to Company

To unleash the power of your company's people and super-charge the focus and efficiency of your organization, you need to coordinate key elements that will enable that process to happen and grow. As I said in this book's introduction, this means building a Constitutional Framework and nourishing a powerful tribal culture that not only engages, aligns and effectively channels the talents of every last employee, but ultimately transcends the company itself to fully encompass and synergize its customers as well.

Yeah, it's amazing stuff, no doubt, but before you get to that, it's always good to take a look back. Why? *Because your history contains the genesis of your culture.*

Your historical narrative culturally unites you and your fellow workers. In fact, too many companies (including ours), especially younger and smaller companies, neglect the importance of everyone knowing their historical and cultural narrative. I will spend more time on the reason why later in the book, but know for now that it is very important. It pulls us together. It defines us.

When it comes to the company that I have been part of for the last 17 years, Ambrose, I find the "look back" to be very instructive, and many other folks have told me that they find it interesting as well. In fact, most people I've spoken to about this subject love the stories from our early days. They certainly contain many lessons learned that shaped the understandings and methodology that drive both our company's success and this book.

So, before I discuss the nuts and bolts of unleashing your company's potential, I thought it would be useful to tell you a bit about Ambrose's history and my own education. Like all ventures, it began with an idea...

THE IDEA

I cofounded Ambrose with John Iorillo in 1996 and the company commenced operations on January 1, 1997. I got the idea from reading an article in the *New York Times* about a failed Professional Employer Organization (PEO) in upstate New York. A PEO provides human resources, payroll and benefits services to small and midsized employers, generally companies employing five to 200 employees. Ambrose is a PEO.

The name Ambrose was suggested by my wife. Ambrose light was a large navigational light tower off Sandy Hook, New Jersey at the entrance of New York Harbor. It provided direction to ships coming toward the safety of New York harbor and warned them to keep wide of the dangerous, shallow Ambrose shoals in the area. As a PEO, this is our job as well, as we provide our clients safe passage and navigational guidance.

I have to give this particular *New York Times* reporter a lot of credit. She actually got in her car, drove up to Albany and found some former clients of this failed PEO. So what happened? This PEO was led by a master salesman, and he traveled around the Albany area selling the PEO concept to many small businesses, but he hated going back to the office and actually running the business.

Obviously, that was a huge problem. So this guy's business lasted for a short time and eventually drove off the proverbial cliff. He didn't take care of healthcare premiums, workers compensation premiums, withholding taxes and other requirements in a timely fashion. The result was a real disaster. His PEO was closed down without advance notice, and all of his clients were left high and dry without payroll, without workers' comp, without health benefits.

Yes, it was a full-blown horror story for the small businesses and employees dependent on this PEO. The story, and the headline, seemed obvious and easy, and many of the local papers in the Albany area reported it in such a way. New York State regulators and legislators in Albany wanted to outlaw the industry. However, this *New York Times* reporter went up to Albany, found former clients and asked "This PEO thing is terrible, right? You're never going to use one again?"

Surprisingly, the former clients generally said, "Absolutely not the case. I will use a PEO again. It was a great concept; I'm just going to find a better, more reputable PEO."

When I read this article, I thought "Wow. There must be a real need and value proposition for this PEO thing." So that is what got it started for me—a *New York Times* article about a failed PEO.

THE LEAP

My founding partner at Ambrose is John Iorillo. We knew each other from New York University's Law School's masters of law (LLM) tax program. We both got our LLM degrees in tax law, which is a post-JD degree at NYU. At the time, I was looking for somebody who was willing to take the entrepreneur plunge. Most lawyers are very risk adverse and not prone to starting these kinds of ventures from scratch, but fortunately, that wasn't the case with John. He was like me, and saw the promise in the PEO idea.

We got started in the Woolworth Building in lower Manhattan in one room, with one window overlooking City Hall Park, two laptops, one desktop (called "the whopper") and a couple of tables from IKEA that we just recently disposed of. I had a friend in the building who was kind enough to let us put a phone on a receptionist's desk. I now call this setup our proverbial "log cabin." *Yes, we got started in a "log cabin"!* (A little story-telling is important.) More importantly, *we had no darn idea what we were doing.* We really didn't. (Current and former clients please note: we were quick learners!)

In those early days, John and I would go to any and every business event in New York. We'd read *Crain's,* one of the city's preeminent business newspapers, going through the listing of all the events and attending every one that we could. We didn't care where in the area they were, and we'd have a competition to see who could collect the most business cards. We would come back the next day and call all of the people we'd met. We worked very long hours, kissed a lot of frogs and faced a lot of rejection. We did this for months, with very little to show, and it was brutal.

AN EARLY CLIENT

What is both interesting and ironic is that despite our ridiculously heavy schedule of events and phone calls, one of our first clients came from the Internet (and this was late 1996). One day that phone on the receptionist's desk actually rang, and it was Jeff Stewart, one of my favorite serial entrepreneurs. Jeff had a 25- to 30-person technology company and was using another PEO. He and his colleagues were dissatisfied with the service they were getting, so he went online, found us and called (I didn't have email at that time). Like the businesses interviewed in that *New York Times* article, he loved the PEO concept but wasn't happy with his current partnership. It just wasn't the right fit for his company.

At the time, I still had my "day job"—practicing law at Brown & Wood (now Sidley Austin) on the 58th floor of the World Trade Center. When the receptionist fielded the call from Jeff, she said we were not in the office at that moment and she'd have us get back to him shortly. She immediately called me up at Brown & Wood, and I then immediately called Jeff.

We set up a meeting in that new, one-room office in the Woolworth Building—the "log cabin." When Jeff and his CFO showed up, they sat down and looked around at the IKEA tables, the "whopper" PC, two laptops, a couple of wooden IKEA chairs and my 1960s-vintage Herman Miller kitchen table from when I was a kid growing up in Westfield, New Jersey.

There was a moment of silence. Then Jeff's CFO said, "Boy, does this office look Spartan."

Our retort was, "Well, that is because everything is electronic."

Nodding their heads, they both said, "Oh, we like that."

THE FIRST YEAR

We did close the deal with Jeff and we started out the first quarter in 1997 with about 35 serviced employees covering two or three clients. (Serviced employees are the employees at our client companies for whom we provide human resources, payroll and benefits services.) Our goal was to get to 100 serviced employees by January 1, 1998.

Despite the early success and a feeling that we were getting some traction, the early going that year continued to be brutal. John and I carried on with our nonstop itinerary and strategy of hitting up large numbers of events and people in New York at that time. There was no state PEO statute codifying our business model, as the industry was still in its infancy and people often asked us, "Is this legal? I don't think what you're doing is legal," or "This sounds too easy and too good to be true."

Our response was, "Oh, yes, we're lawyers, and yes, it's legal." It more or less worked. Our first employee was Marc Dwek (now a principal in Ambrose). He started working for us a couple of days a week.

We did get to 100 serviced employees by January 1, 1998. (As of January 2013, we have approximately 12,500 serviced employees.) In that first year we also closed a deal with a biotech company called Innover, our "hump client" (I thank my late father-in-law, Maurice Hilleman, for that lead), and that put us at about 125 serviced employees after one year in business.

At that point, we had left our six-figure jobs as legal associates at large New York City law firms, and still were not taking home a dime from Ambrose.

As I said, brutal.

From CONCEPT to COMPANY

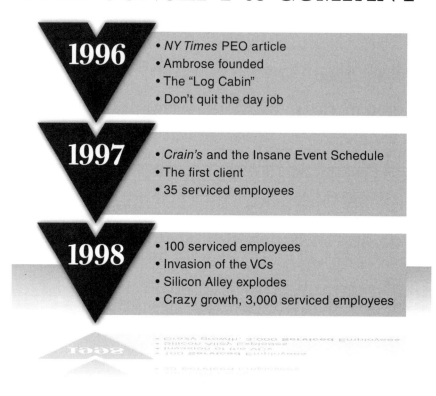

1996
- *NY Times* PEO article
- Ambrose founded
- The "Log Cabin"
- Don't quit the day job

1997
- *Crain's* and the Insane Event Schedule
- The first client
- 35 serviced employees

1998
- 100 serviced employees
- Invasion of the VCs
- Silicon Alley explodes
- Crazy growth, 3,000 serviced employees

The first few years were pretty crazy for Ambrose.

THE RIGHT PLACE AT THE RIGHT TIME

By 1998 we still were slogging along, pitching the novel PEO idea to anyone and everyone. Around April of that year, we got a phone call from somebody who said, "Hi, I just closed my first round of funding, and my VC told me to come down and see you guys. I need benefits, payroll and all that other stuff. Everything. Okay?"

We asked ourselves "Round of funding? What the heck is that?" But desperate for new business (that is an understatement), we did tell him "Sure, come on down."

This was the beginning of Silicon Alley, New York City's version of Silicon Valley. While Silicon Alley was a term that had been coined a few years earlier, this entrepreneurial renaissance had not yet been a visible scene in New York—this was something totally new. These guys—these *kids*—would come down to our office and say, "Here's my check for three million. I gotta go deposit it after I leave here, but I haven't been paid in months, and I have no benefits, and we've just been working nonstop for three months, and we haven't slept so I was just told to come here."

And we're like, "Okay, here's the contract." And they would sign it.

Indeed, the torrent started in April 1998. We had been out speaking to everybody for a year and a half and had little to show for our efforts at this point. But what started to happen in April was unbelievable.

Suddenly, we could not leave the office. We became order takers. The calls from venture-backed startups started coming daily. It was intense. We began to grow at eight to 12 percent per month, and that continued for 36 straight months. That is tripling every year for three straight years. Our first human resource associate was Sean Campbell, who took an early morning bus down from Cornell to interview with us. In 36 months we went from 125 serviced employees to more than 3,000. These dot-com start-up companies had a lot of money and orders to spend it and spend it fast. They were on a mission to change the world. We were the perfect solution for their situation. We accelerated their growth and helped them to focus on their mission.

During this period, it was all word of mouth (more on that later). We would sign up a client, they would have five or so employees and we'd schedule the group enrollment for the following week. We would show up and there would be 30 employees. They would tell friends about us and some of them would leave and start their own companies and call us.

This was a familiar thing in California, but it was very new in New York City. We would sign up clients, and then we'd visit them to do the enrollment and everybody was sleeping on the floor with pizza boxes strewn all over the place. *Sleeping.* We did enrollments where we had to wake the people up from sleeping on the floor.

It was just an unbelievable experience. Commonly—all the time, really—we'd sign up a client with five, 10 employees, and they'd grow to 50 in no time. They had venture money and marching orders to take over the world.

Here is the scary thought: During this time, 85 percent of our serviced employees were with venture-backed dot-com companies. As I said, most of these companies were run by kids (young adults really). We didn't know what we were doing and it really didn't matter because they didn't know what the heck they were doing either. I mean we were just all blind. We were all lost, finding our way. It was an unreal experience but a great opportunity.

When we grew this quickly, it was painful. It was controlled chaos, but we made money and we kept most of it in the business. Our top line would grow every month and our expenses, at that time, couldn't keep up. So net profit grew every month for 36 straight months. That is a nice experience.

We did move offices three times in three years. But our business processes struggled. In fact, we outgrew our business processes within months—they just couldn't even keep up with our growth.

I never want to go through that again. It wasn't the growth that was problematic, but the inability to deliver on our brand promise to our customers. We found it very hard to deliver on a brand promise when we were growing that way, especially when we depended completely on brute force and individual heroics. And, as I discuss in detail later, getting beyond brute force and individual heroics to successfully deliver on your brand promise to your customers is paramount to building an awesome, sustainable business.

So do be careful what you wish for.

2

Finding Discipline After the Dot-Bomb and 9/11

In the late-1990s, Ambrose was on a proverbial rocket ride straight into the stratosphere of startup success, but what followed those 36 months of eight to 12 percent per month growth was the exact opposite. On Friday, April 14, 2000, the NASDAQ collapsed. It closed at 3321; a month earlier, it had peaked at 5133. That affected us significantly. Then the horror of 9/11 occurred, which had a further chilling effect on our collective psyches and our business.

Although this period was painful, we ended up learning many valuable lessons that forced a new level of insight and discipline onto how we defined and ran our company. Ultimately, these lessons formed the development of our *Flip the Pyramid* methodology.

DEALING WITH THE DOT BOMB

When the over-hyped and over-extended Web 1.0 economy began to collapse in 2000, most of our dot-com clients (about 85 percent of our client base at this time) still had some venture capital money on hand, though most had neither revenues nor profits. They weren't going to get any more VC money, but I don't think many of these folks realized that at first. For them, it was business as usual and that meant spending other people's money. However, their investors needed the NASDAQ for their "exit," which for all practical purposes was gone.

The weeks that followed the NASDAQ's crash were silent. We were waiting for the other shoe to drop, and it took a solid three or four months to do so. (We actually continued to grow during the months that immediately followed the NASDAQ collapse because our clients continued to hire.) However, things then changed. We started living through a sharp reversal compared to what we had experienced over the previous three years. We started getting phone calls from our dot-com clients that went like this:

"Hi Greg, this is Bill over at SpendMoney.com." (Yes, the names are fictitious.)

"Hi Bill, how you doing?"

"Awesome, really great."

"Really? What's up, Bill?"

"Ah . . . we can't make payroll."

"Oh . . . why not?" (I knew the answer.)

"We don't have any money."

"Okay. How much money do you have?"

"I'm looking at our account here online, and we have about $930."

"Okay, and how many employees do you have?"

"About 45 people."

"Have you told anybody, Bill?"

"No. No. I can't tell anybody. No way. I love these people, and besides, if I did tell them, they would quit."

"You have to tell them Bill."

"No can do, Greg."

"Bill, you have to hang up the phone and go tell them right now."

"Really? You really think so?"

"Yes. You have to tell them it's all over."

"They're going to feel terrible, Greg."

"Yes, they will."

We received dozens of phone calls like this starting in summer 2000. Seriously. We had a fair number of situations where the CEOs and founders just went home. They just left the building and didn't come back. Some just went home to mom and dad, wherever they were, and they never even told us or their employees!

With absolutely no money in the bank, others talked about the pending "term sheet," outlining their next round of venture capital funding, and that they expected to close on this round "tomorrow." This was unfettered entrepreneurial delusion. We had to help close these companies down. We had to tell the employees it was over. We would also send e-mails telling people it was over. We had people that would say, "I'm leaving now." "Greg, we're out of money." "Sorry." "We're going home." Hang up. Leave the building. Leave their 40 or 50 employees working away in the building.

So many companies ended up with zero money, and we had to go tell them. It was unbelievable. These companies just drove off a cliff. The party for most of them ended very abruptly. Many employees, fresh out of school, were very surprised. They had no idea.

BLACKNESS ON 9/11

After growing at eight to 12 percent a month for 36 months, four months after the NASDAQ collapse our business changed direction 180 degrees. Our revenues decreased weekly. This went on for a solid 12 months and we were exhausted from managing the implosion. It was a big change, and it was rather depressing.

We were already exhausted from the rapid, uncontrolled growth that came immediately before the dot-com implosion, and then had to deal with the dot-com bust. But then things got worse. September 11. This was a dark period for the nation. Eighteen months of losing clients on a weekly basis and then two large commercial jet planes were flown into the World Trade Center several blocks from our offices, killing thousands of innocent people.

On that day, I was in our offices early at 60 Broad Street, talking to a colleague out on the floor overlooking the New York Stock Exchange. (We were located several buildings south of the NYSE.) We heard a very loud roaring noise, a large boom and then there were all sorts of papers flying outside the window (American Airlines Flight 11 crashed into the North Tower at 8:46 a.m.). Our initial reaction was that a company was going public and this was just another one of those celebrations they have down in front of the Exchange. Within minutes, though, the phones began to ring, first reporting that a small plane had crashed into the North Tower. A few minutes later we felt a loud roaring, vibrating noise just above our building (the second jet approaching from the south), another loud crash and more papers flying outside our window (United Airlines Flight 175 crashed into the South Tower at 9:03 a.m.). At this moment, we knew things were not good.

People started showing up for work and reporting total panic down on the streets. I soon received a call from a client who was very concerned because they had several employees attending the Risk Waters breakfast at Windows on the World, a restaurant on the top floor of the South Tower. I told her not to worry because they would be retrieved by helicopter. I was wrong. I did not fathom the towers collapsing— those towers in which I practiced law before cofounding Ambrose.

About an hour later, I was standing in my office on the west side of 60 Broad Street. I heard a loud, deep noise and turned my head toward the South Tower as it collapsed (it collapsed at 9:58 a.m.). I couldn't believe my eyes. It was a horrible sight. This image is indelibly seared into my memory.

We lost 11 serviced employees who were attending the Risk Waters breakfast at Windows on the World that morning. We also lost a very dear friend, Terry Munson, who worked on our workers compensation plan at the risk management company Aon. I had spoken to Terry the day before and recently found a fax from her to me dated September 10, 2001. Terry was the sweetest, nicest lady, and whenever I see a listing of those who were killed on that day, I look for her name. God bless Terry's soul.

After the first tower collapsed, we walked down to the lobby. It was very dark outside because a huge cloud of soot had enveloped our neighborhood. As it settled over everything, the air began to lighten up. And then, another huge roar and within minutes another black plume rolled past the glass front doors and again it was pitch black outside (the North Tower collapsed at 10:28 a.m.). Several prayer circles had formed in the lobby. After the second tower collapsed, we organized groups of people and group captains to start the journey home. When we emerged from the lobby, several inches of fine soot covered the sidewalks, streets and building ledges. An eerie scene.

I live in Manhattan's Upper West Side and the walk home that morning was unreal. The scene was thousands of people in disbelief, trudging in near silence down the middle of New York City's broad avenues. Away from all the destruction and horror, it was a brilliant, clear September day. Sunny blue skies.

Periodically folks would turn their heads to look south in total disbelief, toward the streaming dark plumes coming from ground zero. The twin towers, fixtures of the New York City skyline, were gone, along with thousands of our friends, neighbors and colleagues.

I salute Kim Moore, who worked sympathetically with the families of the 11 Ambrose serviced employees killed on that day to help them through the grieving and acceptance process while she processed their employee death benefits. This was a very hard undertaking. Thank you, Kim.

PICKING UP THE PIECES

From a business perspective, we had battled 18 months of decline and we were now heading into our fall selling season. Half of our new business comes on January 1. Upon completing our fifth year in business, we closed almost no new business for January 1, 2002. Our existing client base continued to hemorrhage.

This was a really dark time. It was as if all commerce just stopped. We went from 3,000 serviced employees in March 2000 to 1,776 in the winter of 2002. We lost slightly less than half our client base in an 18-month period. It was a challenging entrepreneurial experience.

Sometimes you are affected by events outside of your control, as we were here, so I have learned that you must be emotionally and financially prepared for bad events, especially during good times. Bad things can happen quickly, as they did for us, so, my advice is to always be prepared by retaining sufficient capital, keeping debt levels low, and building a strong, healthy, creative and resilient workforce We have since been through the Northeast blackout in 2003, a transit strike in 2005, the financial meltdown in 2007 and Superstorm Sandy in 2012. Bad things happen.

Fortunately, we saved most of the money we made during the dot-com boom, had no debt, and possessed a strong balance sheet for the challenging times that challenged us. (This contrasts sharply with my father's situation when interest rates hit 21 percent during the Carter presidency and his business was forced into bankruptcy.)

We would not have survived this period and we would not be where we are today if we had not been financially prepared. Our solid financial footing helped us to remain calm and focused as we faced these difficult challenges.

SEARCHING FOR DISCIPLINE

By the time 2003 rolled around, we certainly had lots of experience in business and were slowly but surely building our own unique organizational culture. However, we still depended too much on brute force and individual heroics. Organizationally, we were immature and very far from where we are today.

But that's the point at which a key event of our company history occurred and set the stage for the type of transformation I discuss in this book. We learned in 2003 that ongoing growth and success requires discipline that permeates the organization—and yes, such discipline is a pillar of your organizational culture, which I will address in detail in Part Two of this book.

This kind of discipline cannot be gained through a hierarchical command and control or micromanagement approach. As I learned a good five years later, you need an organizational paradigm shift. You need to give employees organizational direction and enable them to self-actualize.

I recently discovered the works of Douglas McGregor, a professor at the MIT Sloan School of Management, who wrote about this subject in his 1960 book, *The Human Side of Enterprise*. In retrospect, I now can fully appreciate the pioneer thinking behind almost all of the great business writers and speakers over the last 50 years. They have taught us how make the crucial paradigm shift that has helped us move beyond brute force and individual heroics to get the best out of each and every person in our organizations.

FINDING OUR FOCUS

Not only did we learn a lot during the dot-com boom and the dot-com bust, but we also had a strong balance sheet. How good is that? We saved for a rainy day, and by 2003 we were damn glad that we had. We did share a few laughs with some of our venture capital friends. What had happened during those previous several years was that these VCs, along with "friends and family," had put money into some very ill-conceived dot-com companies in exchange for some ultimately worthless equity. Some of those VC dollars flowed to Ambrose as fees for services. Rather simple, right?

The thing is, once these VC-backed companies collapsed, the VCs lost their equity investments. We had some of their money as a PEO, but they didn't have any of our equity. A couple of them figured this out and said to us that they should have simply invested in Ambrose. Nice hindsight, but at the time, many considered us just too boring.

We were strong believers in separating core and noncore activities, especially from a macroeconomic perspective. The way we looked at it, these VCs invested in these venture-backed companies, and each of these venture-backed companies could have done what we did internally. They could have built human resources, payroll and benefits expertise, systems and processes within each of these separate companies. They could have hired people to do all this internally, implemented an HR software system, and they could have developed HR business processes. But they didn't.

When they went out of business, from a micro- and macroeconomic perspective all of their internal HR, payroll and benefits processes and expertise would have been disbanded. But those activities were segregated in a separate entity, in this case, Ambrose, and "time-shared" among the VC-backed companies. By concentrating a noncore set of activities in this separate entity, these segregated activities did not go down the drain when the venture-backed companies collapsed. These segregated activities, human capital, processes and expertise remained standing.

From a macroeconomic perspective, this is a very good thing. A business activity that is segregated can easily and quickly be redeployed to serve another sector of the economy (with the employees serving in that separate entity remaining employed). We were free-standing and thus we began searching around for another part of the economy that could use our services. Furthermore, we were built and paid for. So, from a macroeconomic perspective, ours was a significantly more efficient way for our nation's economy to allocate and reallocate human and economic resources.

Around 2003 we witnessed a financial services spin-out and a new startup boom. At this point, the best and brightest, bitten by the entrepreneurial bug glorified during the dot-com boom, started to leave the big financial services firms. This entrepreneurial crowd had the benefit of being able to use an HR, payroll and benefits platform that had already been built, hardened and paid for by the venture-backed dot-com community. Essentially, our new clients, the financial services startups and spinouts, got to reap the economic benefit of what was originally built and paid for by the venture-backed community.

REINVENTING THE COMPANY

Here is a conundrum that we and many other companies have faced: When you're growing at eight to 12 percent per month, you have no darn time to reinvent yourself to stay innovative and competitive, and thereby grow. You're just playing catch-up. You're putting out fires.

During the dot-com boom, we had little discipline around some of our key strategic decision-making. For example, we had no client underwriting or process of any kind to qualify those whose businesses we were considering. We took everyone who came to us. We also had almost no controls over the employees we hired. This ended up creating a mess of both our client base and our human capital.

We were nagged and dragged down by bad, unprofitable customers and tried to solve too many of their wants, both big and small. The loudest, most obnoxious customers set our priorities. This is an exhausting situation in which to find yourself. It's a no-win situation, and gave us our first key lessons:

➢ We needed to define our "sandbox" and to say "no" to a client who didn't fit, especially the loud, obnoxious, unprofitable customer.

➢ We needed to define with whom we would and would not do business.

➢ We needed to proactively and clearly define the needs we would solve.

➢ We needed to become razor-focused on the clients and prospects in our sandbox, get to know them very well to truly understand their needs and then design the solutions that would get them to where they needed to go.

We learned that you just cannot be all things to all people. That is too hard. Do not let the loudest customer develop your business for you. This takes discipline.

It also takes a huge amount of discipline to hire and develop great human capital. Your tolerance for mediocrity must become extremely low. During the dot-com boom, we had no hiring and promotion process in place. We were simply "too busy" to focus on it. We hired people quickly because we just needed bodies, and we handed out "battlefield" promotions regularly (a lot of "Peter Principle" in play). It was as if people were merely cogs in a machine and we had to keep the whole thing running, for better or for worse. From a human capital perspective, we were a mess. Poor behaviors, untruthful gossip, and poor attitudes leading to a lot of poor outcomes and poor service. We also had a lot of petty drama and emotions. What a distracting, exhausting and draining human capital mess. I was responsible for this situation.

We have now learned that human capital is everything. You must become very disciplined around hiring, developing and getting the best out of each and every person. This is an imperative undertaking, but at that point in our history we had put very little time into that task. We ruled by command and control and barked orders. As Professor McGregor discussed in his book, people respond very poorly to this approach. We believed in what McGregor calls "Theory X," that people are lazy and that they need to be micromanaged. Trust me—based on my experience, this is the best way to get the *worst* from your human capital. Our behavior at this time was misery for everyone. We needed to understand and adopt McGregor's "Theory Y," that people generally want to contribute and participate in the great game of business (to steal a term from Jack Stack). We were still years away from this realization but we started to lay the groundwork. We undertook a highly disciplined approach to hiring human capital. This was an important, significant early step.

In retrospect, it is apparent that we were in the middle of a repeating pattern that we ultimately wanted to escape. You want to avoid a pattern like this at all costs. For us, it looked something like this:

➤ We grew and were incredibly busy.

➤ We were always putting out fires (being heroes), and we never had any time to improve.

➤ Our business processes started to collapse under us as we grew.

➤ When we entered an economic downturn, we took the time to start improving our processes, but then we'd grow again, get busy and stop making the improvements.

When the dot-com bubble collapsed, we knew that the economy would come back and that we would find another vertical to serve, so we took advantage of this economic downtime and began to focus on all of our internal processes to strengthen and reorient ourselves.

We were fortunate: Due to our strong balance sheet and strong belief in the value of our business model, we were in a comparatively good place to deal with our weaknesses. We also had the time and energy needed to analyze and improve upon our shortcomings. We had saved a lot of our money during the boom and had no debt.

So we rolled up our sleeves and got to work on strengthening our business processes. We deployed a major software implementation, which was imperative because our old software system had been severely stressed, but most importantly, we focused on the process issues surrounding who we wanted to do business with (client underwriting) and who we would hire to work with us. That was huge. I did not fully realize the positive ramifications at the time.

CLIENT UNDERWRITING: DEFINING YOURSELF

Client underwriting is really about defining yourself—a business process in which you set clearly defined and objectively measurable parameters to define with whom you would do business You define yourself by who you do business with—and don't do business with. This takes discipline. During the period when we were at a nadir in our business, we started an intense client-underwriting process. In fact, we started to turn away customers. We lost almost half of our client base, and we started turning away prospective clients.

We decided we were not going to do business with just anybody. We were looking only for good companies that wanted to be great companies. They needed to be a small business with a good balance sheet that wanted to focus and achieve.

As you might imagine, our sales folks did not immediately receive this development well. We had imploded; the economy was horrible. We were struggling to find new clients, and we rolled out the toughest underwriting process in our industry (and it remains the toughest underwriting process in the industry today). People thought we were nuts. We got a lot of pushback but we wanted to more clearly define ourselves, avoiding obnoxious and unprofitable customers and building a top-tier client base that could withstand economic turbulence. And that is what we did over the coming years. It was one of our smartest moves. This is one of the best things you can do for your human capital; they will love you for this.

Hiring: The Cone of Silence

We had no processes around hiring. This is when we came up with the "Cone of Silence." This meant that all potential hires had to interview with at least 10 people, and no one was allowed to speak to anyone about a candidate. We didn't want group think. Again, it's highly disciplined: Each person filled out his or her own evaluation form and there was group discussion only after all the interviews were done, with all the evaluation forms completed and circulated. Interviews took place with people both inside and outside of a candidate's prospective department.

The reason for this approach was that the people in one's department were more focused on skill set, and people outside of the department could focus on culture and core values. We have always done background checking (and boy do I have stories on that front) and have since added character-trait testing and a very rigorous round of "Topgrading" interviewing (check out the writings of Brad and Geoff Smart), all of which we should have done earlier in our life cycle.

A PLATFORM FOR SUCCESS

By focusing on our weaknesses, shortcomings and outright failures we became more disciplined, increasing the quality of our client base and our human capital. As a result, we improved and strengthened our business processes. We also started to reorient and repoint our platform. Within 24 months of 9/11 we started seeing a deluge of financial services startups and we were ready for them.

However, in retrospect, it's clear that we waited too long to start to develop this disciplined culture and organizational approach to business. Although what I have described so far is just the beginning, we should have done it much earlier. In fact, we should have done it from the beginning. We still had a long way to go at that point. Little did we know, but our journey had truly just begun and there was much more yet to come.

I also realize now that *constant improvement has to happen every single day*, regardless of where you are in your company's development and regardless of whether your business is growing, shrinking or flat. It takes that organizational discipline, accompanied by all of that Jim Collins stuff, which I'll get into in the next chapter, including a Big Hairy Audacious Goal (BHAG—more on this later), core values, annual and quarterly goals, a disciplined meeting rhythm, solid metrics, strong culture, and communication, communication, communication! It involves inverting the organizational pyramid to liberate your human capital to really rock and roll. When this starts to happen, you then really just begin to have fun. That is where we are today and it is awesome.

The moral of our startup story: It doesn't matter how busy you are. You must find discipline in order to develop an organizational structure that allows for you to liberate your human capital, maximize everyone's potential and have fun. That lesson learned, we then began to deliberately learn, explore, experiment with, develop and implement the key methodologies covered in Part Two of this book—all of which are ready for you to put to work in your own organization. We were very surprised at what we learned along this most excellent journey. Let's get started.

Part Two

3
Laying Your Foundation with Core Values

The exciting formative years at Ambrose provided plenty of ups and downs. As I've described, that period also offered an unforgettable learning experience that helped to form the powerful *Flip the Pyramid* methodology. We also practice what we preach.

At its essence, the *Flip the Pyramid* approach revolves around a strong tribal culture. That culture is one of your organization's greatest assets. You build it by establishing a Constitutional Framework, a disciplined meeting rhythm and metric literacy—all of which I explore in the next several chapters.

These tools require consistent, transparent communication and are based on a set of *core values* that require buy-in from every single person in the organization—no exceptions. Our core values are:

- Respect
- Excellence
- To teach and to be taught
- Integrity
- Humility
- Dedication

Getting everyone to embrace and behave by these core values flips the typical company org chart on its head, creating an intense, positive and unique identity that empowers each individual to multiply the constructive flow and execution of ideas. The result: organizational growth and success.

Your core values are your company's behavioral goal posts. Everybody must operate within and embrace these core values. At Ambrose we have all agreed that this is how we are going to interact with each other, and with our clients, vendors, shareholders, stakeholders and the community at large.

This is how we behave, period. It all begins with core values. They are sacrosanct. We have entered into a tribal bond. We agree not simply to act in accordance with our core values, but in a way that glorifies and exemplifies our core values. As an organization, and as individuals, you must live and die by your core values.

Have I made myself clear enough?

BHAG AND CORE VALUES

Jim Collins, author of the bestselling *Good to Great* and other fine books, coined the concept of a "Big Hairy Audacious Goal" (BHAG). We certainly believe in that, and have seriously integrated it with our culture. BHAG is about *horizontal alignment*. It is about the future. It is about everyone being on the same page, moving forward together across the business landscape toward your collective destination. You have entered into a social compact as to where you are going. It is your big goal 10 to 20 years out. It is about focus.

If you think about it, this concept is simple: Everyone stays focused, working toward your company's "true north" while staying within the strict confines of your core values. You cannot cross outside your core-value parameters for the sake of expediency toward your big goal. If you do, bad things will happen (think of Enron, WorldCom). You must remain disciplined and focused.

Core values provide *vertical alignment*—how we behave on a daily basis. It is about today. It is about the present, whereas your big goal is about the future. You are entering into a social compact to behave within clearly defined boundaries. Your core values guide your interactions with each other, with your clients and with vendors on a day-to-day basis.

This is almost too simple, yet very profound. This is very strategic. Now you can begin to let go—to stop micromanaging and liberate your human capital.

SERENDIPITY WITH VERNE

After reading *Good to Great* during Ambrose's formative period, I remained perplexed, asking myself "How do we achieve greatness?" More accurately, the question was, "How do we escape our misaligned malaise?" I agonized over this question for months. Then, serendipity. I had become president of our industry trade association and the executive director had arranged for a one-day presentation by business coach extraordinaire, Verne Harnish. I had absolutely no intention of attending ("Who the heck is this Verne guy?" I asked).

The presentation was on a Tuesday. The Monday before, I got a call from our trade association's executive director asking me if I was coming to D.C. for Verne's presentation. I said no. He said I needed to come because I was the president. Reluctantly, I agreed and the next morning boarded the 6:00 a.m. shuttle from La Guardia to Reagan National, which for me required a brutally early morning wake-up. I arrived at the Ritz-Carlton Pentagon City by 7:30 a.m. and sat at the front table. Verne arrived and started his presentation at 8:00 a.m. sharp. Within 10 minutes I said to myself, "Holy #@*#, this is it. This is what I have been looking for."

Verne was up there describing all of our frustrations in detail—and the reasons for our total lack of direction and why command and control just doesn't work. He pointed out that this is common in organizations. He also explained that there is absolutely no need to figure all this out on your own—that we can all learn from well-vetted, proven business practices and plenty of books and seminars. (In fact, this is how I developed my hearty appetite for business books and attending business and organizational seminars. I now attend Verne's "summits" regularly, and we bring a healthy contingent from Ambrose.)

One point of this digression is that original thinking is not necessary. Many of the concepts I discuss in this book are borrowed. But we've put our own spin on them at Ambrose and have created a few unifying principles of our own. The result has been a supercharged organization. I am proud of this.

....

▼ PYRAMID PERSPECTIVE:
Core Values

By Kim Diorio, Client Services
Fellow Ambrosian since November 2008

Living core values day-to-day within a company can be tough. Sometimes the lines blur between what is and what isn't a core value violation, and making staffing decisions based on core values can, in practice, be a trial. Turning away a candidate who has amazing skills but just doesn't seem to be humble (per our core values) can be difficult in the moment. And terminating an employee—regardless of the reason—is never something we take lightly. It takes a lot of effort to reach the point where everyone in your company fully understands all core values.

Where it becomes even more challenging, though, is holding vendors and clients to those same standards. We consider core values when partnering with vendors and try to get a sense of prospective clients' organizational personalities, but it's tough to get an accurate read on them until we are far down the path of collaboration—typically with a contract in place. So what happens when a client—someone who has agreed to join in the ranks of those who pay your bills and write your paychecks—doesn't fit with your core values? In our case, I give them a good "talking to" and if that doesn't work, we fire them.

As Ambrose's director of client services, I am responsible for ensuring that our clients are happy and that they receive the best service possible. In taking up my role, I've made the deliberate choice to focus on our people, not our service. I know that if our client-facing HR Associates are proud of the company they work for, are treated with respect and concern, and receive the support they need to act autonomously and freely live our core values, amazing service will follow. So I rarely get involved in client issues—unless one of my people is being disrespected.

Most issues that clients escalate are tactical—our platform isn't flexible enough, they received misinformation or they aren't pleased with the response time for issue resolution. Nearly anyone at any level can handle these issues. What is tougher to do, though, is to actively get on the phone with a client and speak to them about treating our employees with respect or, more difficult, terminating the relationship. To do this requires guts, but more important, it requires the support and buy-in from all levels of the organization to follow through on the social compact. The first time I told a client we would not permit them to swear at our associates, my stomach was in knots. I was concerned with how the client would react and in the back of my mind I was wondering, "Does senior management *really* support this—or am I going to be sitting in one of the CEO's offices in a few hours explaining my reasoning?"

By the time I fired a client for the first time, I knew I didn't have to worry about explaining myself. One of our top HR Associates called me after hours, nearly in tears. This was a woman who was rarely shaken. She had just returned from a client meeting where she was humiliated for three hours. The partners were rude to her, blamed her for their own misunderstandings and oversights during the sales process, and publicly swore at her in their office. The choice seemed clear to me. Happily, it was also clear to the sales executive for that client. There have been few experiences at Ambrose more refreshing for me than seeing one of our salespeople willing to forego a commission and a connection with new business in order to support our core values and the HR Associates who work tirelessly to serve the clients they bring to Ambrose.

To say I didn't think twice about insisting that we turn away a brand-new client and new business would be false, but I knew the negative implications of keeping them on our platform would far outweigh any financial benefit Ambrose would receive from keeping them.

Not all clients come equal. Sure, the time and energy spent trying to repair the relationship alone would negate any profits. But the loss in motivation, engagement and enthusiasm of one of our top employees would have been far more costly to our company financially and in terms of our Constitutional Framework. We terminated the client the next morning and haven't looked back, except to reflect and realize that perhaps we increased the commitment of that employee and helped her rest easier that night knowing that her manager—and the rest of the company—had her back and would follow through on our espoused core values.

TRANSCENDING MICROMANAGEMENT

The morning after my original Verne Harnish encounter, back in New York City, I sat at my desk thinking about how disconnected we were at Ambrose. We were arguing all the time, over the facts and over our direction. Analysis paralysis. It was an organizational disaster. We were also micromanaging. No one knew where we were heading, so we had no choice but to micromanage, which felt horrible for the micromanager and for the micromanaged.

Have you ever micromanaged someone? How did it make you feel? Have you been micromanaged? How did *that* make you feel? Do you think micromanagement makes you more or less productive? I am sure we all agree on the answers.

Micromanagement is a killer. Surveys indicate that 79 percent of workers believe that they have been micromanaged, with 71 percent reporting that it has interfered with their ability to perform their job.

(I actually find these percentages unbelievably low.) This startling fact is made all the more troubling by the fallout it causes: preventing most organizations from attaining optimal success, and in many cases, preventing them from attaining any success at all.

Micromanagement stems from leadership's failure to build the organizational structure that enables people to self-actualize in an aligned, engaged and empowered manner. Micromanagement saps precious energy from all members of an organization, from client-facing employees to the CEO. It keeps everyone bogged down as mere toilers, spinning their wheels while achieving, at best, only small steps forward. Micromanagement diminishes people, makes them feel terrible, and provides for a poor return on an organization's human capital.

Back in the day, we wanted to stop micromanaging because it felt horrible, but we were afraid that doing so would set us adrift. You may feel the same way.

So what is the solution? On one hand, you need to stop micromanaging, but then, on the other hand, you also need to provide an organizational framework for direction and management.

AN ORGANIZATIONAL FRAMEWORK

An organizational framework starts with what I call your "Constitutional Framework"—a set of values and expectations that provide a guiding force for everyone in the company. We decided that we needed to do that, but for us there is never a straight road. We took a detour, but did finally get there.

When I returned from meeting Verne I spent some time thinking about how we were going to implement change—to implement the proven business practices he had discussed. The trick was implementing change without creating analysis paralysis. I knew people were going to think I was drinking some Kool-Aid and would ignore me if I started blabbering away, so instead of talking about it, I decided to try to implement some small changes first. I knew we were going to change slowly and incrementally at first and, I hoped, build up momentum, which is exactly what happened.

CREATING CORE VALUES

Our core values already existed to some extent in our culture, but they were not codified and so they were not as strong or visible as they should have been. Senior management agreed that we needed to raise their visibility to near-sacred status, so we began to analyze, define and formalize them.

We argued for nine months over our core values. Wordsmithing. Total analysis paralysis—and this was one of the detours I mentioned. I fully expected this. Soon everyone dreaded the regular meeting where we would get together to work on this matter.

After nine months of frustration and pain, I suggested a coach. This idea brought a collective sigh of relief because we all were exhausted by this time. So guess who I called?

I contacted Verne Harnish and told him we needed the best coach he had. He sent us Roger Merriam. We started at 8:00 a.m. on a Monday. By 10:00 a.m. our core values were done. We were stunned. By lunch we had completed our additional building blocks of core purpose and our brand promise, which I discuss in detail in the next chapter. We finished our BHAG shortly after lunch and then worked on our annual goals. We accomplished so much in one day that we unanimously decided to have Roger come back every quarter. We are still using Roger's services today.

Having a coach, and more importantly codifying our core values, changed our lives. We saw a way to let go, to stop micromanaging without setting ourselves adrift.

WALKING THE TALK

Core value violations are very, very serious. As an organization, you must take your core values seriously. If a core value violation isn't taken seriously, your core values are meaningless.

When there's a core value violation, there's a flag on the field, play halts, no compromises. You must talk the talk and walk the talk. Enron talked the talk but didn't walk the walk.

I like to ask people the following question: "What happens if you

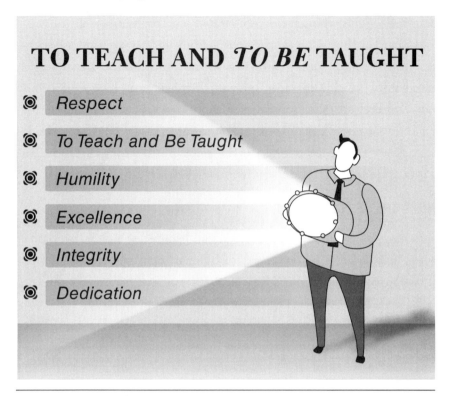

TO TEACH AND *TO BE* TAUGHT

◎ Respect

◎ To Teach and Be Taught

◎ Humility

◎ Excellence

◎ Integrity

◎ Dedication

Core values are your company's behavioral goal posts.

have an A player on the skill set side of the equation—your best, top performing salesperson—but that person commits a core value violation? What do you do with that person? The answer is simple. He or she needs to exit the organization. Unfortunately, we have had to do this, as I'll illustrate in a moment (yes, we have made hiring mistakes). What is good about codified core values that are alive and well is that real violations are generally clear and obvious. There is nothing arbitrary about core value violations.

It is also clear when people do things that are excellent examples of your core values. As leaders, you must constantly look for these examples and praise them and hold them up for everyone to see. You must constantly bring your core values to life and give them depth and breadth.

At our quarterly company meeting, where I am allotted about 20 minutes, I spend considerable time shouting out and reading stories about individuals who have demonstrated our core values over the previous quarter. They get a raucous cheer from the crowd. This is leadership. You are never done emphasizing your core values. Every single person must be able to rattle off your organization's core values and know that they are taken seriously. Without core values, you run the risk that your corporate culture will evolve toward *Lord of the Flies,* toward the dark side of human nature. Several steps in this wrong direction are a serious emotional drag on your company's ability to perform.

WHEN THERE ISN'T A FIT

Right after we codified our core values and started to talk to everyone about them, I had a fellow in our tech department come to my office to speak with me about our core values. He was technically very skilled. He said, "Greg, I've been thinking about these core values and they are not me." I asked him to explain, and he was correct. He did not fit with our core values. I told him that I could see where he was coming from, and he then said that he needed to leave the company. I told him I agreed and thanked him for his honesty. We clearly "mishired" this person, but still had ultimately achieved the right outcome.

After our core values were more firmly rooted, we had another person in the tech department, also very technically competent, who wasn't fitting in. His colleagues looked at our core values and decided he was not a fit and so they asked for us to fire him. We call this "being voted off the island by your peers." Basically, he was served up to management for discharge due to a core value mismatch. We were merely the messenger.

We met with this person and presented him with our core values—Respect, Excellence, to Teach and to be Taught, Integrity, Humility and Dedication—and told him that we didn't think that he shared them with us. He looked at the list and said he respectfully disagreed. He then said that he had Excellence, Integrity and Dedication, gave examples and rested his case. We agreed with him on those three, but then asked about Respect, to Teach and to be Taught, and Humility.

He opined that having all six was an unreasonably tall order. I told him that I didn't know about that, but that at Ambrose you need all six. We then told him that he didn't have Respect, that he had treated his peers with contempt. We also told him that he wasn't humble, that he had been acting like someone who thought he knew everything. Finally, we pointed out to him that he wasn't willing to teach or learn from others.

He agreed and then mumbled something about breaking eggs to make an omelet. We told him we weren't in the omelet-making business and that accepting all of the core values was how we behaved at Ambrose. At this point in the conversation, he knew the outcome. He wasn't a cultural fit. He needed to leave. The decision was easy.

Unfortunately, I could give you a few more examples along these lines. While we interview for core values, and are upfront about them from the beginning, we do make mistakes, as will you. However, if your core values are alive and well, violations and mismatches will be apparent in short order. Then you must take action.

Cultural guardians and others will feel empowered to step forward and put a flag on the field, especially when they know leadership takes core values very seriously. You need a culture that is vigilant on this front. No exceptions. Ever.

Your core values must be stronger than the ego of any one individual and must be strong enough to eject a malfeasant C-level employee. As a shareholder in Ambrose, I feel that our core values protect my investment. However, a broader way to look at it is as a *stakeholder*, whether as an employee, client, vendor or shareholder. Incredibly strong core values protect the interests of all stakeholders. You do not depend on any one individual to protect the organization. Instead, you have a strong cultural value set that serves the purpose.

We have faced unfortunate situations of value mismatches. It can happen. It will happen. Dealing with violations hasn't been pleasant, but our core values have ultimately prevailed. You must strengthen your core values to the point that they are capable of standing up to, and overcoming, any malfeasant individual irrespective of where he or she is in the organizational chart. Core values are part of an organization's foundation and leadership must constantly emphasize and discuss core values so that they achieve a high level of vibrancy.

▼ PYRAMID PERSPECTIVE:
Team Trumps All

By Christopher Gaine, Sales Professional
Fellow Ambrosian since March 2012

I left my first Ambrose job interview knowing something was different about this company but I just couldn't put my finger on it. The questions I had been asked were atypical for the first round. While few questions focused on my experience and skill sets, many probed me as a person. As I pondered my answers, I quickly realized that while skills were important, team was obviously more important to this company. Actually, at Ambrose team trumps all. If you don't play well with others, you don't play at all.

To many people this realization may be daunting, especially when you look around the room and see a bunch of twentysomethings. How could these people possibly be my peers? I have more work experience than many of them have years. Still, I experienced the realization of new beginnings and opportunity.

For the previous 11 years I had worked in the financial industry, where loyalty trumped intelligence, fear was instilled early, creative thought was squashed and there was no questioning who was boss. A great story to illustrate this point is that on my first day of trading, I was made to sit beside the senior trading manager on the desk. Approximately 30 seconds prior to the open we received a large buy order for a stock and I was told to control the stock market open at 9:30 a.m. and purchase stock smartly—"don't pay up, but don't miss it." I had no idea what any of that meant.

By 9:32 a.m. I was getting blasted in my right ear and being told that I would never amount to anything, that I "sucked" and that I was to sit there and not touch anything, especially my keyboard. For the next three minutes, the stock traded higher and my boss did nothing but make me watch as he chewed me out. Every few seconds he would tell me how much money I had just lost the firm because enough volume had traded that he owed the customer a fill lower.

I protested and told him that if he had not told me to sit on my hands, I could have purchased most of the stock order at a lower price and the purchase report would have looked great. Apparently, that was the wrong thing to say because once again he was screaming at me—this time literally to the point of him spitting on me with each word.

Within 10 minutes of the start of my first day, I was told that I was worth nothing, I had cost the firm $50,000 and I should say goodbye to an end-of-year bonus. I wished I had never left my old company for this place.

For the next 11 years, Wall Street remained much the same. Despite my eventually "getting it" and performing extremely well to the point of becoming a senior person in the group, I was subjected to constant managerial oversight and chest pumping by people with loftier titles who left me desiring more. Apparently, I wasn't alone; what was once a desk of 126 people had dwindled to fewer than 20 and most of them were looking to leave at their first chance.

What made those 11 years a particularly painful experience was the fact that prior to coming to Wall Street I had worked for a firm that was highly collaborative, innovative and rewarded failure as much as success. People were not afraid to think outside the box, try new things or most importantly not always play it safe. I had seen the other side of the coin and desperately wanted to be part of it again.

Leaving my initial interview at Ambrose, I felt that I had found just what I desired.

CHAPTER SUMMARY

Core values are the cornerstone of your successful organization and its constitutional foundation. Your core values are your company's behavioral goal posts. Everybody must operate within and embrace these core values.

Main chapter points include:

➤ Core values require buy-in from every single person in the organization—no exceptions.

➤ Ambrose's core values are Respect, to Teach and to be Taught, Humility, Excellence, Integrity and Dedication.

➤ Getting everyone to embrace and work by core values multiplies the constructive flow and execution of ideas while fueling growth and success.

➤ A constitutional foundation based on a set of values and expectations provides a guiding force for everyone in the company and helps you avoid micromanagement.

➤ You must hire for fit to your core values, and when somebody does not abide by them, they must exit the company. Everybody must "walk the walk" with no exceptions.

This is the first step in letting go—of inverting the organizational pyramid and unleashing everyone's creative energies in an aligned manner. This is the organizational paradigm shift that is necessary to avoid micromanagement, which is so diminishing and destructive.

In the next chapter, I address how core values, brand promise, core purpose, BHAG and quarterly and annual goals combine to form a Constitutional Framework that will negate the need for micromanagement, enabling your talented employees to flourish in the pursuit of success.

4 Creating Your Constitutional Framework

In Chapter 3, I discussed how core values create a social compact that defines behavior, attitudes and expectations within clearly defined boundaries. Your core values guide your interactions with each other, and with your clients and vendors on a day-to-day basis. When you combine these core values with goals, you create a situation where everyone is focused on, and working toward, your company's true north, what Jim Collins calls your "Big Hairy Audacious Goal" (BHAG). You cannot cross outside your core-value parameters for the sake of expediency toward your big goal. If you do, bad things will happen (think Enron or WorldCom.) They require that you remain disciplined and focused, which obviously is a very good thing.

At Ambrose, we have created an organizational structure that combines our core values with goals. This structure helps all of us figure out on our own, and with our teams, what we need to do to reach our individual, company and departmental goals, providing tribal guidance. I call this structure our *Constitutional Framework*.

You give people direction by building a Constitutional Framework. They know where they are heading. No misunderstandings, no ambiguity, no micromanagement necessary. People become dependent on the organization's Constitutional Framework.

Think about that for a second. *No micromanagement.* With a Constitutional Framework, everyone in the organization has a general roadmap for getting from today to tomorrow without any unnecessary oversight or misguided direction from others. It's about power and self-actualization. It's where the proverbial rubber meets the road in flipping your pyramid and igniting the potential of everyone in the company, driving progress forward toward the BHAG.

Combined with incremental goals, core purpose, brand promise and a tribal mentality—all of which I describe in this chapter—this approach becomes very powerful indeed. Additionally, having this framework reduces infighting and internal politics, especially when collaboration and teamwork are required to successfully move forward.

WHAT'S YOUR BIG, GRAND GOAL?

Everyone in your organization must understand and focus on the company's true north, your "Big Hairy Audacious Goal," or BHAG. Our BHAG is:

Ambrose is recognized nationally as the best provider of HR solutions to small businesses.

It doesn't matter exactly how you state your BHAG as long as everyone in your organization understands where you are trying to go. Everyone must know the journey's destination. This goal must be one that cannot be achieved through any single individual's heroics; if it can, then it isn't grand enough. No one person can get you to your BHAG. It must require a tribal (team) effort. People love, and are united by, grand goals, so you must give your colleagues a grand goal. It is part of the tribal experience. It is also fun for all to be part of something big. This is human nature. This is strategic leadership.

In 1962, President John F. Kennedy gave the United States a very grand goal: to put a man on the moon by the end of the decade. As a nation, and as individuals, we were all excited, united and focused on this goal. We did indeed achieve it when Neil Armstrong and Buzz Aldrin walked on the lunar surface in July 1969. During that decade, across the United States, teachers taught, and students learned, with this grand mission in mind. We were all inspired and aligned toward this big goal. It united us.

Not long after President Kennedy had laid out this grand goal, he visited the space center at Cape Canaveral. While there, he happened to encounter a worker, a janitor, with whom he had a brief chat. Kennedy asked the worker what he did at the space center. A bit surprised by the question, the janitor responded, "Mr. President, I am helping to put a man on the moon!" That was the correct answer, and that is the type of response you want from everyone at your company. *Everyone's* goal was to put a man on the moon. Now *that* is strategic leadership.

▼ PYRAMID PERSPECTIVE:
The Importance of Goals

By Steven Caldwell, Technology Programmer and Analyst
Fellow Ambrosian since September 2012

Goals are important. Goals matter. Setting and achieving goals, both for the individual and for the company, makes a difference. When a company sets realistic annual goals (long-term goals for an individual) that will be broken down into attainable quarterly goals (short-term goals for an individual), then the big tasks that seemed insurmountable suddenly become surmountable.

Imagine a sailboat with its sails unfurled. The forces of wind and current cannot keep that ship from its destination. This is what it's like to have goals. Now imagine that same sailboat lowering its sails. Now it is subject to the forces of wind and current, and it may never reach its destination. This is what it is like to not have goals. In my opinion, a company or an individual that does not have goals is just like a ship adrift.

Prior to my arrival at Ambrose I worked in technology at the same company for 14 years. The company was a very large, multinational corporation with more than 10,000 employees around the world. From an outsider's perspective, there was no reason for my wanting to leave. I was compensated well and received a robust benefits package. But I was unsatisfied with my position, and that began to carry over into my personal life.

The problem was that the company I used to work for had no "real" annual goals—at least nothing that was well defined. Yes, they sent out an email stating something along the lines of "grow the business" and "reduce costs," but that was it. No follow-up. No explanation to the individual employee regarding how they would contribute to reaching these goals. Without any real annual goals, there could not be any real quarterly goals. Eventually this worked its way down to my department not having any goals at all. How was I supposed to feel engaged knowing that what I did had no impact on where the company was heading?

I was just like the sailboat with its sails lowered. But instead of being buffeted by the forces of wind and current, I was subjected to the attitudes of "just keep the thing running" and "we want it done as quickly as possible." For those of you unfamiliar with technology workers, while we understand that it is our role to support the business of the company, we really want to know that the company supports us.

After my first round of interviews with Ambrose—which was rigorous to say the least—I walked out puzzled. I wasn't sure what had just happened, but I knew that it was certainly different from my previous 14 years. As my conversation with Ambrose continued, I began to learn more about their goals and how they went about achieving them. Ambrose didn't just pay lip-service to the idea of having goals. Ambrose did not send me an email with a cut-and-paste message. I learned that Ambrose has *real,* attainable annual goals, and they go about reaching them by first achieving smaller quarterly goals. These quarterly goals are simply the annual goals broken down into realistic components.

This understanding became clearer to me as I onboarded with Ambrose. My manager allotted time for me to learn what Ambrose does, and how Ambrose separates itself from other companies in its field. I recognized that a goal at Ambrose is to bring new team members along at a pace that enables them to really understand what the company is doing. This was a new experience for me. For the first time in my technology career, I felt like I was a part of something. I wasn't simply an employee number, but a person who had skills to help Ambrose achieve its goals. Going forward, I know that achieving my personal goals would help my department achieve its goals. That in turn would help Ambrose achieve its goals.

Although I have been a member of the Ambrose team for only a short time, I can say that I am no longer that sailboat with its sails lowered. Ambrose has helped me to once again raise my sheets to the wind. Now, whatever force of wind or current comes my way, I know that I will be able to stay on course and reach my destination.

SETTING ANNUAL AND QUARTERLY GOALS

Your BHAG is your organization's ultimate focus, however ambitious. So how do you reach it? You do so incrementally, using annual and quarterly goals. These are more concrete.

As Verne Harnish likes to say, "A company with too many priorities has no priorities." This is so true. Individually and organizationally, we can put only so many tasks or goals on the front burner. This means that your organization must set and clearly communicate its priorities if it wants to clarify its goals. Everyone in the company needs to know your priorities in order to tactically work smart, creatively and efficiently.

Goals are about focus, horizontally aligning all of your daily activities. Each set plays into and supports a higher set. Here's a sample hierarchy:

> A company's **BHAG** is the ultimate goal.

> Four or five company-wide **annual goals** point to and support the BHAG.

> Four or five company-wide **quarterly goals** point to and support the annual goals.

> Departmental **quarterly goals** point to and support the company's quarterly goals.

> Team and individual goals align with departmental quarterly goals.

These quarterly and annual goals should be objectively measurable, with no subjectivity or ambiguity. (I discuss creating a metric-literate culture in Chapter 6.) Here we also have found it helpful to tie variable compensation to these objectively measurable goals. Everyone must know and focus on these goals, and variable compensation provides a gentle reminder of these goals (always be careful when relying solely on extrinsic motivators such as compensation). You must create goals every quarter. No excuses. But remember, first you need your BHAG.

▼ PYRAMID PERSPECTIVE:
Annual and Quarterly Goals

By Annie Abbondante, Office Assistant
Fellow Ambrosian since May 2012

We all know the cutesy adage, "Shoot for the moon. Even if you miss you'll land among the stars." This might make a great high school yearbook quote, but it's not exactly an ideology that works in business. If you shoot for the moon and miss, you might land among the unemployed and penniless. In itself, blindly "shooting for the moon" is a dangerous strategy.

At Ambrose, our BHAG is "Ambrose is recognized nationally as the best provider of HR solutions to small businesses." It's an objective that Ambrose strives to attain on a daily basis. Each member of the tribe at Ambrose knows this goal and actively works toward it. Because of our communal culture, we believe that our personal successes collectively create Ambrose's success.

Nevertheless, however ambitious the BHAG is, it's virtually unattainable without a detailed plan. If each year or quarter we simply measured ourselves against that goal without first having a methodical roadmap for attaining it, we would all be in constant despair and disarray. It's virtually impossible to become "the best" without steadily working one's way to the top with a detailed plan.

Recently we decided that the Ambrose office in New York was looking dull and didn't represent the company well. We wanted our office to reflect unquantifiable attributes such as "fun," "pretty" and "comfortable." We knew that an office make-over was a big project, and that not many people had extra time to dedicate to a project that large. It would have been great if remodeling could have just been done overnight, but of course that wasn't realistic. There was too much we wanted to do to just have it all happen at once. So, a few representatives from the various departments at Ambrose decided to devise a plan.

We met to evaluate exactly what things we would need to do for us to get what we wanted. We broke down our wishes (a fresh coat of paint, nicer art on the walls, new lighting fixtures, a revised conference room floor plan), and also set priorities and time constraints. That giant, indistinct idea of "Let's have a nicer office!" suddenly became a doable, definitive objective with clear, delineated action items. And when we got each phase of the project done, we enjoyed the results so much that we gained momentum and enthusiasm to continue working.

We upgraded our maintenance contract, got the carpets steamed, and the windows washed. We chose a paint color and hired a painter. We consulted with a furniture vendor and had our errant conference room rearranged into something more functional and streamlined. Our employees created and donated beautiful art to hang around the office. All of a sudden, we found ourselves turning our office into what we wanted it to be, and it wasn't nearly as insurmountable or complicated as we originally had thought.

At Ambrose, we create the company we want to work for in the same way. We produce our own progress by formulating, setting and sticking to annual and quarterly business goals. This helps us to celebrate smaller wins and successes rather than dwelling on the fact that we did not become "the best" overnight.

We set strategically aggressive yet attainable goals each year. Each quarter, we set up smaller initiatives, which we refer to as "rocks," that help us get to our annual goals. Breaking things down even further, we create monthly, weekly, and even daily goals to keep ourselves aligned and on track. Because of this, each person in each department can very specifically define how they personally will move Ambrose toward its BHAG. At the end of each day, after working hard and getting tasks done, each individual at the company can say, "I helped Ambrose move toward our BHAG today!" These are quantifiable, concrete examples of how each person makes a difference in the tribe.

It's really a rather simple concept: We take baby steps. And those little steps add up. At the end of the year, when we review our progress, we can see how far we've come, both personally and as a company. Using these set goals and rocks, it's easier to plot out our successes and failures, determine what we should do differently and identify our next steps.

Our next steps become our new annual goals, and so on. In this way, we are constantly moving toward well-defined intentions. We work together, which helps foster a strong culture of invested employees. Everyone knows his or her role and what is expected of him or her. We are driven forward by a sense of purpose, rather than each person attempting to become "the best" by forging ahead on their own, working sightlessly toward an amorphous goal.

An Ambrose-revised version of the "Shoot for the moon" motto would be, "If we all take baby steps, we'll eventually get to the moon. Together."

DEFINING YOUR CORE PURPOSE

In addition to developing core values, a BHAG and annual and quarterly goals, you also need a defined core purpose. This is what your company does best. Your core purpose also helps the organization stay focused and keeps you from running astray. For example, this is Ambrose's core purpose:

To enable small businesses to focus on their *core purpose.*

Everyone knows that everything we do must be aligned with this core purpose. All tactical actions must align with and strengthen your core purpose. It's easy for everyone to overlook the organization's core purpose, so, as with the rest of your Constitutional Framework, leadership must constantly articulate the company's core purpose.

CREATING CUSTOMER ALIGNMENT WITH BRAND PROMISE

Brand promise is the last (but not least) piece of the Constitutional Framework, exclusively dedicated to that all-important stakeholder, your customers. Brand promise aligns everyone with your customers, and everything you do must align with your brand promise. Here is Ambrose's brand promise:

Great people, great solutions, and great delivery.

We work for our customers, and this is our promise to them.

As a leader, your job is simpler than you think. It is to develop your Constitutional Framework and make it vivid, to bring it to life. Everybody has to know your core values, BHAG, annual and quarterly goals, core purpose, and brand promise. This is a huge part of a leader's job. It's not tactical micromanagement. This is strategic leadership. As soon as you get out of the tactical day-to-day and shift your focus to your Constitutional Framework, individuals will maximize their participation and grow, your company will grow and everyone will have fun to boot.

In fact, you must get to the point where people start to say, "Oh, no, here we go again, talking about core values…" You need to talk about this stuff until you just get a smile on people's faces and they know exactly where you are going. Wash, rinse, and repeat. No surprises.

Think about what you are doing here. Leadership puts an incredible amount of time and energy into building a Constitutional Framework. Everyone then enters into a social compact, agreeing to the Constitutional Framework, and also to transparency and a lot of communicating. At this point leadership can totally let go of tactical reins to let company employees have an incredible amount of freedom and creativity within this construct. Enable everyone to participate in a meaningful way. People want to put that man on the moon. It is human nature—the intrinsic satisfaction that we all crave—so build the framework. Give everyone an excellent experience. This is strategic leadership.

▼PYRAMID PERSPECTIVE:
Our Core Purpose

By Dave Zodikiff, Chief Information Officer
Fellow Ambrosian since June 2012

When I interviewed at Ambrose I immediately felt the connection between my own journey and the company's journey. I had been working at Whole Foods for 11 years and had come to embrace the idea that an organization's core values, core purpose and brand promise are essential in shaping how it acts, and equally important, how its employees act.

For me, these concepts helped shape the guiding principles I used every day to make decisions. As I looked for my next role, I wanted to ensure that I worked for a company that supported this ideal. The more team members I talked to at Ambrose, the stronger that commitment felt. Ambrose's core purpose is "To enable small businesses to focus on *their* core purpose." I translate this to mean our core purpose is to take away all of those daily tasks that are not helping you do your job, so you don't need to think about them.

Today, faster, smaller and more accessible devices are standard. People pick up their iPhones or iPads and instantly download the latest songs or buy amazing applications for $2.99. Our business partners, clients and customers should expect the same from us. The old days, when the IT (technology) group could hide behind the "wonder" of technology, have disappeared. One could even argue that they have flipped.

Most people expect technology to be simple and immediate. Our IT group focuses on figuring out how to meet those expectations. That's where our core purpose comes into play. We no longer should be focusing on WOWing our users. We need to develop intuitive systems so that they can get in quickly, get what they want and then get on with their own core purpose. The user's experience has become one of our primary areas of focus.

One way to better understand our core purpose is through a football analogy. IT is the offensive line. Our job is to block and protect the other players so they can gain yards and eventually score. This job isn't for everyone. It truly takes a special breed of folks. We know that many kids dream about being the star quarterback who throws the touchdown pass, or the running back who spins and leaps past tacklers on the way to the goal line. But we all know none of that would be possible without an offensive line. This is true in business as well. We need the offensive line. As an IT professional, I am proud to be one of them, clearing the path for the rest of the team to score.

AMBROSE'S
CONSTITUTIONAL FRAMEWORK

◎ **Your Core Values**

Respect, to Teach and be Taught, Humility, Excellence, Integrity, and Dedication.

◎ **Your Big Hairy Audacious Goal (BHAG)**

Abrose is recognized nationally as the best provider of HR solutions to small businesses.

◎ **Your Annual and Quarterly Goals**

A company with too many priorities has no priorities.

◎ **Your Core Purpose**

"To enable small businesses to focus on their core purpose."

◎ **Your Brand Promise**

Great people (service, knowledgeable, responsiveness, cultural fit)

Great solutions

Great delivery

Your Constitutional Framework features several important concepts.

RELYING ON TRIBAL GUIDANCE

If your folks all know your core values, your BHAG and your annual and quarterly goals, then as a leader, kiddingly, I like to say, "I can go home. Why do they need me, right?" Folks know what to do. Everyone can make tactical decisions and take steps that align with your Constitutional Framework.

Here is a typical scenario for someone looking for guidance: A colleague comes to leadership to discuss a tactical action. Frame the discussion within the context of your Constitutional Framework. Ask the following:

"Is the proposed action consistent with our core values?"

"Is it moving us toward our BHAG, our annual goals, and our quarterly goals?"

This is the basic analysis. After you go through the exercise a few times, people will stop coming to leadership for this sort of tactical advice. They can do this on their own or with their peers, provided your Constitutional Framework is vivid and clear. Leadership is then liberated to continue to focus on the strategy and the company's overall BHAG. Leadership is liberated from a tactical morass. For your own mental health as a leader, and for the mental health of everyone else in your organization, this is huge—it helps you obtain strategic clarity and tactical alignment.

So the idea here is that nobody needs to come to leadership to make a tactical decision. Everyone looks to your core values, your BHAG, and your annual and quarterly goals to figure out the right choice. Folks are codependent on your company's Constitutional Framework; folks are not codependent on senior level leadership for tactical direction.

However, my earlier statement about leaders going home is a joke because you cannot underestimate the importance and amount of work necessary to make your Constitutional Framework vivid. It takes a significant amount of leadership, especially in the beginning, when the framework is not clearly defined or ingrained or when your business starts to grow and you start adding new people and opening new offices.

START NOW

Do not wait too long to start building your Constitutional Framework. In fact, my advice is to start building your Constitutional Framework, and the required organizational discipline, from the beginning. At Ambrose, we waited way too long to do this. We had been in business for 10 years before we really built out our Constitutional Framework. We had gotten to about 35 internal employees and we were stuck in the mud with a lot of micromanagement. We depended on the individual heroics of a few hard workers and we were exhausted.

This is important: The first 10 years of business *without* a strong, vivid, clearly defined Constitutional Framework were very, very hard. We relied on brute force. Once we built our Constitutional Framework, growth commenced with speed and with aplomb. We quickly paced to more than 100 employees and profits dramatically increased. By comparison, the last six years in business with our well-defined and promulgated Constitutional Framework have been much easier.

I think you should remain borderline paranoid about your Constitutional Framework. It should keep you up at night. It is never vivid enough. Always think about what you can do to strengthen your Constitutional Framework, to make it more vivid. This is a never-ending journey.

ASSURING TRIBAL ACCOUNTABILITY

While a company's leadership must spend considerable time and energy developing and communicating its Constitutional Framework, it is equally important to make sure the tribe holds itself accountable. That is, everyone must be held accountable for behaviors and tactical actions to make sure they align with the company's Constitutional Framework. Leadership should not micromanage, but folks should self- and team-manage by constantly looking at the company's Constitutional Framework.

A good leader is a bad micromanager. A bad leader is a good micromanager. However, you cannot avoid micromanaging unless you have built a solid Constitutional Framework and the organization is willing to hold everyone accountable (although you do need a tolerance for failure, something I will discuss later).

Your Constitutional Framework is your strategic, management framework. What you must require from everyone is that their tactical actions align with it and that they exhibit total transparency. No one is to toil away in the dark. This is a big part of the puzzle. This is the agreement; this is the social compact.

ARE YOU ROWING OR SAILING?

Here's an analogy I like to talk about: *Are we rowing together or sailing together?* I think rowing together is a bad analogy for business because it implies that we're all doing the same thing. The coxswain yells "row, row, and row" and everyone rows. Sailing, if done right, is very different.

I like to race sailboats (www.TeamManitou.com). We generally have eight folks on the team, and it is a very complex sport. When we race on my boat, we have three goals that everybody knows: have fun, be safe, and cross the finish line first.

We also have core values. When you race a sailboat, each person has very different responsibilities. It is a total team sport (and one that you can play as you get older). The skipper cannot engage in heroics and try to micromanage the boat. This is a losing approach. The classic, yelling, micromanaging skipper is a loser (and the crew despises him or her). The skipper needs to focus on other tasks, particularly overall strategy and steering the boat. The skipper has a tactician, the chief operating officer so to speak. The tactician works with the crew on coordinating and executing maneuvers that align with the team's strategy. The skipper cannot micromanage tactics and still do his or her job. If the skipper tries to do this, bad things will happen.

A tactician and a solid crew will strategically execute without the skipper's involvement. This is how you win on the water and in business.

In fact, I love to show up at races and compete against the skipper who thinks he or she is the smartest person on the boat. The proverbial screamer. Nobody wants to race with this person, so he or she usually must hire a professional crew. Not an inexpensive endeavor. These folks are professional sailors, and yet they usually lose. They're sitting up on the rail, this paid crew, saying, "What do you want me to do? Yeah, okay." The skipper screams and yells at them and afterwards they don't want to hang out with the skipper. No team work; no alignment. They have no vivid vision. No excitement to win. No tribal connection. They are micromanaged by the skipper. It's an organizational disaster.

I never yell. I have a great team. Everybody executes. When there are problems, the crew figures out the solution and tells me when it's fixed. They fix it. I can't focus on it. They figure it out. Everybody on the boat is smarter than me (A players hire A players and B players hire C players). And, yes, we have a Constitutional Framework for Team Manitou and we review our Constitutional Framework before and after every race. Everyone is liberated to confidently take tactical actions consistent with our Constitutional Framework and there is no need for "leadership" to micromanage. In fact, "leadership" has been liberated as well, and now can focus on the bigger picture.

Remember: individual heroics cannot get you to your big goal. If individual heroics can get you to your goal, your goal is not big enough. Conversely, everyone wins when your entire team is managed by a vivid Constitutional Framework. Everyone is then liberated to focus on and participate in getting to a really big goal. This is how you win. Beat your competition, and achieve big things. This is how you put a person on the moon.

CHAPTER SUMMARY

Your Constitutional Framework combines your core values with goals, core purpose and brand promise. This structure enables all of us to figure out on our own, and with our teams, what we need to do to reach our company and departmental goals—with no misunderstandings, no ambiguity, no micromanagement.

Main chapter points include:

> ➤ With a Constitutional Framework, everyone in the organization has a general roadmap for getting from today to tomorrow without unnecessary oversight or misguided direction from others.

> ➤ A Constitutional Framework is about power and self-actualization, flipping your pyramid and igniting the potential of everyone in the company to participate in a meaningful way.

> ➤ Everyone in your organization must understand and focus on the company's Big Hairy Audacious Goal (BHAG).

➤ You attain your BHAG through meeting annual and quarterly goals on multiple levels.

➤ Your core purpose helps the organization stay focused and prevents it from running astray.

➤ Buy-in to your brand promise assures alignment with your all-important customers.

➤ Your Constitutional Framework negates the need for tactical micromanagement, as long as everyone's tactical actions align with it.

Building and maintaining your Constitutional Framework is just the beginning. You must bring it to life. A disciplined meeting rhythm keeps it alive. You also need to create a metric-literate organization, a tribal culture, obsession with communication, embracement of change, acceptance of failure and dedication to personal growth—all covered in the following chapters. When you do all of this, you unleash your human capital. There is no need for command, control and micromanagement. Your tribe will be engaged, empowered, aligned and on fire.

5

Establishing a Disciplined Meeting Rhythm

Building your Constitutional Framework takes time, dedication and experimentation. However, simply constructing that framework is not enough. You have to bring it to life with a disciplined company-wide meeting rhythm.

Meeting rhythm is the communications backbone that keeps everyone connected and aligned with your Constitutional Framework. It is the system by which everyone is constantly vetting, in a very transparent manner, their tactical actions against your goals, core values, brand promise and core purpose. Regular meetings at several different levels are indispensable. They enable you and your employees to observe, understand and steer the dynamic growth of your company every single day. They help you to answer the questions, "Are our tactical actions aligned?" and "Are they moving us toward our goals?"

MORE DISCIPLINE

The meeting rhythm consists of dailies ("daily huddles"), weeklies, monthlies and quarterlies. These meetings do not belong to any one individual, nor do they depend on the presence of anyone in particular. These meetings belong to the organization, to the tribe.

This is an important point to communicate. The tribe does not amount to any one person, particularly to the heroics of any one individual. If I am not around, or if I'm out of town or late, it doesn't matter. All meetings start at the same bat-time, same bat-channel. We have a meeting "captain," but if the captain isn't present, someone else steps in and runs the meeting, which provides leadership opportunities for others.

The meeting schedule is set in stone for the year. Every person at your company should be in a daily, monthly, weekly and quarterly meeting.

This is worth repeating, and takes discipline as well. The meetings and the rhythm are not owned by senior management. They are owned by and serve the organization. If I am absent for a month or two, the meetings continue unabated and without a hitch (I sometimes wonder if anyone would even notice my absence). Here, senior leaders and managers need to learn to stand down, check their egos. These meetings are not about them.

A regular meeting rhythm dramatically increases the flow of information through the organization, fosters teamwork and tribalism and provides for alignment, focus, tempo, accountability and transparency. There are a lot of eyes on everyone's tactics. No one is allowed to toil away in the dark.

Meeting rhythm also fosters collaboration. It is a structure that each person and team can tap into to get guidance on their tactical actions. In fact, you should get to the point where everyone is getting ideas from others in respect to their tactics whether they ask or not. The meeting structure facilitates an easy and efficient flow of ideas.

This must become the norm. We have found the return on a disciplined meeting rhythm is huge. For us, a disciplined meeting rhythm that belongs to the tribe is a game-changer, especially when it isn't owned and dominated by the "smartest person in the room."

INSTALLING THE DAILY HUDDLE

Back in 2008, during the period in which I was grappling with my initial concepts of alignment, I approached the head of our Human Resources Services group and explained to her the concept for the "daily huddle" and how these meetings would be critical for leveraging and aligning everyone. I also emphasized that this was not my idea, but that many successful companies were doing dailies. This approach turned out to be the first proven alignment practice that we implemented, and it has been key to our success.

When I met with the HR leader, I explained that these daily huddles are about ten minutes long, every day at the same time, and everyone stands in a circle briefly announcing what's up and what is the irritating rock in their shoe. There is no problem-solving at the daily; problem-solving *follows* the daily. I gave her some literature on "dailies" and showed her a video of Verne Harnish describing them. She thought it was a great idea and agreed to experiment with them.

After two weeks, she reported back that the dailies were a huge hit. Folks loved them. They brought everyone together on a daily basis. The dailies gave people the opportunity to raise issues every morning—not just their issues but client concerns as well. Problems were identified and resolved more quickly. If an issue remained at the end of the day, it was raised again the next morning. They didn't have to hunt someone down to discuss an issue; there was a daily, scheduled slot for discussion. This alone saved a lot of time.

Other departments soon heard about the dailies and asked if they too could give them a try. It became viral and in short order the whole company was doing them. Around this time I recall sitting in a senior executive meeting when one person asked, "What are these dailies?" I responded, "They started with HR Services, worked well, and now everyone is doing them and just loves them. Why don't we do one as well?"

We have been doing them ever since. They are organizationally set in stone. Every person at Ambrose is in a daily every day. No exceptions (unless, of course, you are on vacation or sick). The dailies cascade "upward" (I use this term reluctantly), so after all of the operating group dailies, one person from each operating daily calls into the management daily.

Some dailies are face-to-face (with some folks joining by video conference) and some are dial-ins. They happen at the same time every day.

They start on time, and they end on time. No waiting for anyone. This is also about being disciplined and not dependent on any one individual. This is an important message.

REAL COMPANIES DO DAILIES

Real companies do dailies. Cara Wright worked for Ambrose before we started dailies. She left and went to Target, where everyone already was in a daily. At Target, they too conducted dailies that cascaded from the store floor to the executive suite in Minneapolis, Minnesota every single day. When she came back to Ambrose (something we celebrate), she was very excited to hear that we were doing daily meetings as well.

The White House does dailies. In fact, I have heard that they do twice-a-day dailies, and that they cascade up. Ritz-Carlton also does them. There the room-service personnel attend dailies. I often take the first flight down to D.C. for meetings at the Ritz-Carlton, and on numerous occasions I have seen staff engaged in these meetings. At the Ritz-Carlton they flow all the way up to corporate headquarters.

Once you start doing dailies, and are disciplined about them, everyone will love them. No one person can dominate the daily; everyone must participate. You cannot achieve alignment without a good flow of information and active participation by everyone. I wish we had done this from the beginning, as our growth would have been a lot easier.

Dailies are easy to implement, an easy quick hit, and prove indispensable. They were the first part of this larger construct that we implemented; even before we codified our core values.

Dailies allow for "stucks" to efficiently flow through the organization. If you think about it, when a client-facing employee has a stuck, is it really his or her stuck or a client's stuck? The dailies make it possible for a client's stuck to be voiced on a daily basis. There's no running around trying to escalate an issue. Instead, a daily structure lets everyone access more experienced, knowledgeable and creative team members.

EAR TO THE GROUND

On occasion, I get a telephone call from an early client with an issue (someone I "closed" and/or even enrolled years ago). The call almost invariably starts out, "Hey Greg, sorry to bother you with this and I am sure you are unaware of my problem…" Almost always *I am* aware of what's going on because the issue has cascaded to me through the dailies. Thanks to that, I am able to respond, "Joe, I am aware of the situation. I don't have the answer, but we have been putting resources on the problem and are working very hard at coming up with a solution. In fact, it was raised in our dailies yesterday and this morning and will be raised again each day until we resolve your issue." I then get a "wow" and we proceed to have a 10-minute discussion on dailies and the value of a disciplined meeting rhythm. How cool is that for customer service?

As this story illustrates, the dailies also let client issues flow freely through the organization; client issues are not trapped with your front-line workers, leaving management in the dark. This free flow of issues aligns the whole company with your clients. This is just one way that the voice of the customer can penetrate through the organization on a daily basis. I find it refreshing when the whole company hears a customer's voice on a daily basis. It is a nice reminder about who we are working for.

Dailies are about discipline and alignment. They are easy, visible, effective and a great way to lead change. Dailies help ally your whole organization with your brand promise. If you are not already doing dailies, give them a try. You will not be disappointed.

▼PYRAMID PERSPECTIVE:

Daily Huddles

By Marvelle Roberts, Human Resources
Fellow Ambrosian since April 2006

I remember the first day that we were told about the daily huddle. Sean Campbell, my boss at the time, circulated a great article called, "The Daily 'Adrenaline' Meeting." After reading this clipping, I distinctly remember being in shock that there were companies out there that actually put their employees through torture by having a standing meeting every single morning.

I thought to myself, "Shouldn't they be working? That's just wasting time." At that point in my career, I was an HR Associate who felt like there was never enough time to get all my work done in one day and here I was given yet another meeting to attend. You can imagine how anxious I felt having 15 minutes of my day taken away from me. I thought the only positive thing about this was that we were told that it was just an experiment and that if the meeting exceeded 15 minutes, we had the right to walk out. I thought, awesome! I've got an out.

After just a few days of huddling around, the unthinkable happened. I fell in love. What I didn't realize was that I became a lot more aware of what was going on within the company. I started learning of the issues that were affecting my peers. We were substantially smaller then, so our huddle comprised of multiple departments, including legal services, benefits, HR Services, and operations. We slowly started learning the pain points that each other had and when a theme kept recurring, we knew we needed to develop a process to fix things.

Remarkably, we started getting things done at a faster pace and started to communicate with each other better. The other thing that happened was I found myself interacting more with my peers because while we didn't necessarily solve issues during huddle, different groups of employees would have impromptu mini meetings, right after the huddle to discuss and often solve an issue that was brought up just minutes ago.

It was great. No longer was I left to work out issues on my own. I felt like I had an entire team of individuals willing to help me before I became frustrated with a problem. I also became more sensitive to the needs of my colleagues and knew which projects they were working on. Also, if someone was overwhelmed, others quickly offered to lend a helping hand.

> To this day, on their first day of work, each newly hired employee receives a copy of the same article I received. We've since incorporated recognition into our dailies, which adds a little more fun to our morning diet.

WORKHORSE WEEKLIES

Weeklies are very tactical and operational. They should have a running agenda. Everyone should have the opportunity to report on what he or she has been working on and to engage in informed discourse.

This is also a great forum to review department-level metrics. A lot of PowerPoint presentations, metrics, discourse and brainstorming. These meetings provide the perfect opportunity to get constructive input from your peers on your projects. This is the workhorse meeting at which you review your department's key metrics and the metrics for your area of responsibility.

Again, management cannot dominate these meetings, but needs to facilitate discussion and involvement by everyone. If you haven't already read it, I highly recommend Patrick Lencioni's book, *Death by Meeting*, to help you and others in your organization run a positive, inclusive, comfortable session.

Weeklies are very, very different from dailies. Dailies are very short; dailies are informational. There is no problem-solving in dailies. Weeklies, on the other hand, are longer and more in-depth. They too, however, must meet at a regular time each week.

Remember: Weeklies are also about organizational discipline. They facilitate an in-depth review, problem solving, brainstorming, and discussion of tactical undertakings. Often one or several members make a formal or informal presentation on an issue or project accompanied by informed, intelligent discourse by all attendees. An important goal of the weekly is full engagement by all members.

To simplify: Weeklies generally serve two purposes. First, they provide an organizational overview of the team or department for the week. This purpose helps to prioritize who is working on what. Second, they provide feedback, brainstorming and collaboration on tactical undertakings to make sure they align with the company's strategic goals and Constitutional Framework.

MERRY MONTHLIES

Our monthlies are company-wide. They last about 20 to 30 minutes and take place at various sites using the video-conferencing service GoToMeeting. They are quick, fun and to the point. In monthlies we review our annual and quarterly goals in light of their key metrics. We indicate whether we are green, yellow or red on our goals. Green means we are meeting our goal (super green means we are exceeding our goals), yellow means we are a bit behind our goal and red basically means we are failing to meet our goal. At minimum, the monthlies provide an opportunity for the whole company to pause, look up, think about our annual and quarterly goals, and assess our progress toward them.

We also go over the status of all of our initiatives, including where they are in the development cycle. We end the meeting by celebrating new hires, birthdays, anniversaries and anything else we can think of, particularly new product launches, promotions and significant milestones.

You need some celebration, and yes, it is tribal. The monthly has an unbelievable effect on aligning us. After each monthly, everyone knows where we stand with respect to our annual and quarterly goals (especially if we are behind!) and is aware of all the cool tactical developments that are happening all over the company.

Our monthlies recently have evolved into a rather entertaining and comical "radio" show. The live commentary that goes with the slide presentation has a lot of funny banter among the folks who "produce and broadcast" the monthly along with their "special guests" from throughout the company. People love our monthlies.

COOL QUARTERLIES

What I find very cool is that every quarter every department gets to show off what they've done to move us toward our quarterly and annual goals and our BHAG. This is exciting. It provides leadership opportunities and high visibility for recognizing successes. These quarterly meetings aren't dominated by senior management. They too are fun, participatory and tribal.

Our quarterly meetings are a bigger production than the monthlies. They can push two to three hours, but they are well worth it. In our quarterlies, each department has the opportunity to show everyone what they accomplished that quarter. This leads to some fun competition among departments, which strengthens communication.

Information flows. Each department presents its quarterly achievements and failures through a presentation to the whole company. They pick their own presenters, so this provides some great opportunity for folks to develop their presentation and public-speaking skills. (We also have a presentation coach come to Ambrose to run workshops for our employees.)

A week before each quarterly, you cannot book a conference room at Ambrose. Folks are holed up all over the place practicing their presentations. On quarterly day, presenters come in with their spiffy clothes and fresh haircuts. A lot of pride, some jitters and excitement. It is really awesome. People cheer for the presenters and for all of our achievements. It is very tribal. Of course, they give me only 20 minutes. What do I talk about? I talk about our Constitutional Framework.

Core Value Stories

When people think of a core value, I want them to think of particular individuals, so in advance of a quarterly meeting we collect stories from throughout the company about individuals who have exemplified our core values during the previous quarter. I stand up in front of everyone and read as many of these stories as I can in 20 minutes, bringing our core values to life, giving them meaning and context.

Everyone cheers when I share these stories. Here is just one, recent awesome story I read at our quarterly:

Alex is a payroll all-star. As a team lead in the payroll department, she does a great job supporting her team as well as the HR Associates. I have seen her again and again take extra time to explain a task to a new hire, and go above and beyond to find solutions for our clients.

I can't tell you how many times I have heard a HR Associate say that she got on a call, clarified a question or helped smooth a difficult client interaction. Respect, dedication, teach and be taught—Alex embodies all of Ambrose's core values.

Everyone feels great, not just the person named in the story. This is one of my favorite tasks at Ambrose. In fact, I did it once several years ago, with no intention of doing it every quarter, and in advance of the next quarterly, people started stopping me to ask if I wanted their stories. I just love doing this! Core value stories are tribal. They reinforce our social compact.

In one quarterly we held a costume contest and all presenters wore costumes. That was fun. So order some noisemakers. Buy confetti. Have fun. Push yourself as a leader into the goofy, uncomfortable zone. The truth is, as humans, we love this stuff. We are tribal animals.

▼PYRAMID PERSPECTIVE:
Quarterlies

By Christine Pesaturo, Retirement Plan Group
Fellow Ambrosian since April 2003

Ambrose's quarterly meetings are amazingly successful, but they weren't always so. The quarterlies were originally a forum for our senior management team to provide updates to the rest of the firm. The problem was, by the time our quarterly meeting came around, some of the news was old and the majority of employees weren't engaged. Our quarterlies weren't focused on our goals or a particular theme. We didn't include an Employee of the Quarter award, relevant metrics, noisemakers or stories of outstanding employee dedication.

Then one day, the senior management team asked each department to present at the next quarterly meeting. We were given very little guidance, just the instruction to share what our team had been working on. I think this is when the quarterly buzz and excitement began.

Most presenters, me included, didn't exactly deliver a captivating presentation the first time. In fact, it was downright boring! Many of us missed the mark on the metrics we presented because we failed to explain why the metrics mattered to the firm. Perhaps we missed it because we were inexperienced presenters and out of our comfort zones. We were nervous to present to our bosses and peers. A lot of us had shaky knees and sweaty palms, and our presentations were filled with awkward "ums." I read directly from the PowerPoint slides to avoid eye contact with the audience. Some presenters even spoke at the pace of an auctioneer!

At that point, I understood why public speaking was the number-one fear among people, followed by a fear of death, heights and spiders. Jerry Seinfeld's famous gag about the fear of public speaking resonated with me. Seinfeld joked that people attending a funeral would rather be lying in the casket than delivering the eulogy.

The good news is that the fear didn't last long. We learned to sharpen our presentation skills through constant practice and feedback to find what Greg Slamowitz refers to as the "presentation zone." It's the state where the presenter has *captured* the audience—the people in the chairs want to hear what the presenter has to say next.

Now we present with excitement and in our own unique style. Those projections of our voice and smile reflect our enthusiasm and the audience affirms it with nods and cheers. We still have room for improvement, and I'm sure the meetings will continue to evolve in various ways, but I'm impressed with how we've grown as individuals and as a tribal organization.

THE POWER OF RHYTHM

I cannot emphasize enough the game-changing effect of a disciplined meeting rhythm. Thanks to our structure of regular meetings, individuals from throughout the organization are constantly connecting with each other, their group and the company. They are constantly connecting their activities with the organization's quarterly and annual goals. Everything is always in context. Everything is clearly tied to a defined and well-understood objective.

As I mentioned earlier, building your Constitutional Framework is the beginning. But you cannot end there. A disciplined meeting rhythm keeps it alive. You also need to create a metric-literate organization, a tribal culture, obsession with communication, embracement of change and acceptance of failure, and dedication to personal growth. Once you do this, you will find that you can let go and unleash your human capital—your organizational pyramid will be inverted. You will have no need for command and control and micromanagement. Your tribe will be engaged, empowered, aligned and on fire. I discuss the importance of creating a metric-literate organization in the next chapter, and share a few good stories as well.

CHAPTER SUMMARY

Just devising a Constitutional Framework isn't enough. You must bring it alive with a disciplined company-wide meeting rhythm, the communications backbone that keeps everyone connected and aligned. Regular meetings at different levels empower you and your employees to observe, understand and steer the dynamic growth of your company every single day.

Main chapter points include:

➤ Everyone must attend daily, weekly, monthly, and quarterly meetings.

➤ A regular meeting rhythm must become part of your organizational fabric.

➤ You keep your meeting rhythm alive through discipline—these meetings must happen on schedule, despite whoever is or isn't there to lead them.

➤ A regular meeting rhythm provides leadership opportunities.

➤ A regular meeting rhythm improves communication.

➤ A regular meeting rhythm strengthens your Constitutional Framework.

➤ A regular meeting rhythm aligns strategy and tactics.

➤ Have fun with your meetings. They are key to building your tribal culture.

In the next chapter, I discuss how to build metric literacy among your employees. Understanding and becoming comfortable with metrics is another essential support component of your Constitutional Framework and organizational (tribal) alignment.

6 Building Metric Literacy

As I discuss in previous chapters, flipping your organizational pyramid to unleash the full potential of your employee talent requires building, developing and continually strengthening your Constitutional Framework. That essential, governing structure is itself made up of core values, brand promise, core purpose, a disciplined meeting rhythm, quarterly and annual goals, as well as what author Jim Collins calls a Big Hairy Audacious Goal (BHAG).

However, there's another key element to making it all work. You also need metrics. A *lot* of metrics.

Like the disciplined meeting rhythm, metrics bring your Constitutional Framework to life. In fact, metric literacy is a critical component of organizational (tribal) alignment. You cannot invert your organizational pyramid and liberate your human capital without metrics and a universal understanding of what they're telling you about your company's performance. It is like being in a stadium playing a game of baseball with everyone being acutely aware of the score, who is at bat, the number of balls and strikes, and who is on base. And more. This is what you need to achieve. Everyone needs to keep an eye on the score, so you need a scoreboard.

BILLY BEANE AND JOHN HENRY

Metric literacy provides you with an advantage over your competitors who may have more money and resources, but don't have an ingrained Constitutional Framework, don't have a disciplined meeting rhythm, and don't focus on metrics. If you haven't done so yet, read Michael Lewis' book, *Moneyball: The Art of Winning an Unfair Game,* and watch the movie. In case you didn't know, the book and movie address the amazing tale of how Oakland A's baseball manager Billy Beane was able to make the most of the Major League's lowest payroll. With an innovative and disciplined use of metrics, he turned his team into a top contender, even against large-market teams with millions of dollars more to spend. It's a fascinating true story, whether you're a sports fan or not.

Moneyball has a lot to teach us. Near the end of the movie, John Henry, the owner of the Boston Red Sox, wants to hire Beane away from the A's to join his organization. I found the verbal exchange between them to be very telling on multiple levels:

Billy Beane: Well, I was grateful for the call.

John Henry: You were grateful?

Billy: Yeah.

John: For $41 million, you built a playoff team. You lost Damon, Giambi, Isringhausen, Pena and you won more games without them than you did with them. *You won the exact same number of games that the Yankees won, but the Yankees spent $1.4 million per win and you paid $260,000.* I know you've taken it in the teeth out there, but you're the first guy through the wall. It always gets bloody, always. It's the threat and not just the way of doing business, but in their minds it's threatening the game. But really what it's threatening is their livelihoods, it's threatening their jobs, it's threatening the way that they do things. And every time that happens, whether it's the government or a way of doing business or whatever it is, the people are holding the reins, have their hands on the switch. They will bet you're crazy. I mean, anybody who's not building a team right and rebuilding it using your model, they're dinosaurs. They'll be sittin' on their ass on the sofa in October, watching the Boston Red Sox win the World Series.

[He takes out a paper from his coat pocket and puts it in front of Billy.]

Billy: What's this?

John: I want you to be my General Manager. That's my offer.

[Billy takes the paper and reads the offer then looks back in shock at John.]

While Billy Beane did not accept Henry's offer, Henry did adopt Beane's obsession with metrics and went on to break the curse of the Bambino and win two World Series Championships—after an 86-year drought.

I love this exchange because it validates Billy Beane's metrics-driven approach to baseball, but also because it highlights that being the first is hard. The real winner, John Henry and his Red Sox, were followers. You don't have to be the first to win. As I have said before, the business practices described in this book contain little or no original thinking. Followers can win. No shame necessary. I am simply describing proven business practices and how they have had a radical, positive impact on our experience in the practice of business. Metric literacy is a proven business practice. Everyone in your company needs to learn how to think about what gets results and what needs to be measured.

▼PYRAMID PERSPECTIVE:
Liberation through Metric Literacy

By Josh Newman, Marketing and Product Development
Fellow Ambrosian since May 2004

Metrics are liberating. Just the thought of metrics calms me because with good metrics I feel confident about what I'm doing and the decisions I'm a part of. In business, we call it metrics, but in life it's billed as "information"—and no one doubts the benefits of that.

As the director of a new marketing and product development team, I find the use of metrics to be critical. Ambrose did quite well without a marketing team for more than a decade, and thus adding this area of the company was met with some hesitation. Cognizant of this, the marketing team built out our metrics early on, not just because they are necessary for marketing, but because we knew we had a to be transparent about our performance and contribution to our departments and the company's key performance indicators (KPIs).

We needed to achieve buy-in and to extricate ourselves from debates void of real data. Those debates are not liberating, and certainly not calming. As it turned out, the activities that the marketing team developed spiked web traffic and inbound lead flow, two of our KPIs. As soon as we made this "information" transparent, it established credibility for the department and garnered respect from the company that our team was in the best position to design and execute effective marketing activities. Ah, liberation!

Before we made our metrics transparent, our team was pulled in many directions. Everyone seemed to have the "best" idea for us, ranging from guerilla campaigns to ads on airplane radio programs. The team remained disciplined by pursuing campaigns focused on digital and thought leadership. Meticulous measurement and reporting of these campaigns liberated us. Fast-forward less than two years and we've more than doubled lead flow and web traffic.

The use of metrics has had a similar effect on our team members. The new marketing team was largely built with internal Ambrose employees, rather than pulling in talent from outside. Consequently, the team was composed of A players passionate about Ambrose culture, but green on traditional marketing experience. This team thrived under Ambrose's Constitutional Framework, as we voraciously read up on best practices and ran small measured experiments on what we learned. Obsessively measuring and reporting gave us the confidence to experiment.

This contagious confidence democratized our idea generation, leading to a quick learning curve and development, and a quick improvements in results. Without metrics, it would have been a challenging environment for the less experienced members of the team to contribute so strategically. At this point, metrics are so interwoven to the team's fabric that we use Moneyball as a verb, as in "Let's Moneyball this new campaign!"

Managers are faced with decisions all day long, and making decisions is mentally exhausting. This is particularly true for decisions with incomplete or no data. The flow of good information eases decision-making, lets more people participate in decision-making and yields smarter decisions. Ultimately, in an optimal informational environment (lots of relevant metrics), I find that I'm freed up to spend more mental energy on the most important thing: people.

WHAT'S THE SCORE?

Visible metrics focus the whole company on its quarterly and annual goals. Every goal, every project and anything you want to improve should have at least one metric. The metrics tied to your annual and quarterly goals are your most important organizational metrics and are called your key performance indicators (KPIs).

These are your most important metrics, and they should be leading indicators (remember that your quarterly and annual goals must be objectively measurable). What I mean by this is that if you hit your KPIs, and if you hit your goals, you should similarly hit your lagging indicators, your key financial metrics.

Your key financial metrics are not your key leading indicators. Financials are generally a look in the rearview mirror. They tell you how you did last month or last quarter or last year. Because your financials tell you where you were, they are considered lagging indicators and are woefully inadequate to provide you real-time guidance as to where you are and where you are going. For this, you need solid, leading KPI!

This is an absolute requirement. Your leading KPIs tell you how you are doing today. You cannot run your company using financials alone—too often the information it provides would be too late to enable you to make corrective, tactical course corrections.

Everyone, and I mean everyone, must know and watch the KPIs for the company, their department and their projects. They must be reviewed at least monthly (in the monthly meeting format discussed in Chapter 5), although my preference is for KPIs to be viewed weekly or daily in a transparent manner.

As an example, in 2012 Ambrose's top four goals, and their corresponding KPIs, were as follows:

➤ A targeted client Net Promoter Score (NPS), which we measure quarterly and average for the year.

➤ A targeted additional new client (new sales) serviced employee head count.

➤ A targeted client retention percentage.

➤ A targeted per serviced employee productivity/profit improvement.

All of these goals were identified before the start of the year together with their associated KPI targets. Everyone in the company knows these goals and their associated KPIs.

Something I have been encouraging that we have not yet done is to display scoreboard screens in all of our offices that show our annual and quarterly goals, the current metric readings, and an indication of whether we are red, yellow or green on each goal. (Our Business Intelligence group is busy working on this now.)

Hey…it's just as though you were in a stadium playing a game.

Everyone needs to know what the score is at all times, not just senior management. You want total transparency around your goals and your metrics. This provides everyone with knowledge of your progress toward your goals and keeps people totally focused on your company's priorities. Everyone needs to concentrate on and engage in the "game." You need the whole team (I do prefer the word tribe) to know the score at every play in order for everyone to perform their best. How can you ask or expect people to get into the game, play their best, and enjoy it, if they don't know the rules and are not following the score?

METRICS:
Are You Moving Towards Your BHAG?

◎ KPIs

◎ Metric literacy

◎ Ownership

◎ Self-management;
are tactics working?

◎ Data rather than tradition,
whim, hearsay or anecdote

Metrics are essential to activating your Constitutional Framework and avoiding micromanagement.

TACTICAL METRICS

Transparency around your KPIs also gets people comfortable with metrics, and teaches them that everything that they do, their tactical undertakings, also need to have a metric. Metrics are for everyone, not just for senior management. There is no need for subjectivity regarding our overall strategic progress or department, team and individual tactical progress. Let's agree on the goal, the metric, and objectively measure our collective and individual progress.

This approach simplifies things. It removes a lot of drama, uncertainty, and anxiety. *It isn't you; it's the data.* Metrics also provide folks with a tool for easy and constant self-assessment. *Don't come to me and ask how we are doing; just look at the metrics. Let's go to the scoreboard.*

In a metric-literate organization, you will find that people self-correct very early in the process. *People have a tool to assess their tactics. You tell me if your tactics are working.* In this environment, people will know if their tactics are working, further negating any need for micromanagement. This is a nice thing.

START NOW

I strongly recommend that you get serious with metrics right away. If you're not already focused around metrics, start now. Looking back, I believe that it took too much time for us to create a metric-literate organization. We didn't have metrics for our first 12 years in business, except for lagging financial and some presales data, which is typical for many businesses. We were arguing over whether we were achieving our strategic goals and tactical goals because we had no darn idea what they were or where we were on our journey.

Quite simply, we didn't know the score. We were frustrated, so I read Jack Stack's book, *The Great Game of Business,* and travelled to Springfield, Missouri for his seminar. (Although not the easiest travel destination, I highly recommend that you do the same.) I was thoroughly impressed with what Stack had done with metrics in a manufacturing setting. Thousands of hourly employees had become metric literate and were having fun using those metrics to make tactical improvements. They were successfully moving Springfield Remanufacturing Corp. strategically toward its objectively measurable goals. There were scoreboards on the factory floor. Everyone had to learn metric literacy during orientation. It was a totally metric-literate company. Very impressive.

▼ PYRAMID PERSPECTIVE:
Rising Above Micromanagement

By Jim Andrews, Accounting and Finance
Fellow Ambrosian since September 2011

The revolution was ancient history when I arrived "in country." The Constitutional Framework that once propelled an overthrow was the well-established rule of the land. All citizens were aligned and thriving under this new regime.

This insurrection was not televised or found on the front page of any newspaper or website. As you might guess, this was not an event on the geopolitical landscape, but the cultural revolution of a growing company, Ambrose. The nation's citizens were its employees. The tyrannical reign of micromanagement, misery and "misaligned malaise" was toppled by an entire workforce empowered with weapons such as daily huddles, core values, goals, KPIs and metrics.

Ambrose uses metrics and KPIs to measure and track every aspect of the business. From revenue and expense drivers, hiring statistics and operation volumes all the way to employee appreciation events—every activity Ambrose engages in gets a meaningful metric assigned to measure and be managed. What a concept!

I'm a classically trained accountant, Certified Public Accountant and all-around "numbers guy," so the uses of metrics and KPIs were in my wheelhouse. It had been my experience that these tools were generally housed in company departments such as finance and accounting. But at Ambrose, I was shocked that all, *and I mean all*, employees were expected to be versed in and use KPIs and metrics as a tool to manage the company.

As I attended my first daily, weekly, monthly and quarterly meetings I was stunned by the pervasive and rampant use of metrics. Positions not traditionally oriented in numbers, such as internal human resources and the events planning staff, were reporting their activities and results via metrics. Graphs, charts, numbers and trends replaced the standard bullet-point phrases and long-winded narratives on PowerPoint presentations.

The liberation of this nation was evident by the use of metrics. Guesswork and emotion no longer aid in determining results. Decisions and discussion are enabled by facts that lead to meaningful and creative dialogs. The population of this

> nation is forever emancipated from micromanagement with the armament of two powerful weapons: metrics and KPIs.
> *¡Viva la Revolución!*

OUR METRICS STORY

As I mentioned earlier, we were a little late to the metric literacy game. We finally introduced metrics across our company when we had about 40 employees. It was a very emotional experience for some people, something I fully failed to anticipate.

I thought if Jack Stack could do it, surely we could easily do it in a white-collar setting in lower Manhattan. Did I make a mistake? Here is what happened.

For 12 years, we were having problems with answering our phones. For 12 years customers complained they couldn't get through. Our Net Promoter Score (NPS) clearly indicated that this remained a big issue for them. Senior management thought we knew the answer and we dictated this and that for years. It usually amounted to simply getting stern with people to answer the phone. Hmm . . . that didn't work.

I decided that we needed to try a different approach. *Let's just put up a couple of scoreboards with some inbound call metrics and then ask the front-line folks to figure out how to improve the metrics, how to move the needle.* We told them that they had to figure it out, and that our clients asked for this to get done (they were aware of this because everyone had been reading through the NPS comments). We had never made this sort of request of folks in 12 years in business. This was a first.

Nevertheless, it seemed rather simple and logical.

At this point in my learning, I had not read any of Professor John P. Kotter's books, such as *Our Iceberg Is Melting* and *Leading Change,* which focus on achieving buy-in to new ideas and processes. (Professor Kotter is a must read.) So what happened? The scoreboards went up and people revolted. It was very, very emotional for some. I was accused of micromanagement. Senior management was watching everyone, they thought.

People thought they were going to be fired if they didn't improve the numbers. One person was so emotional that he threatened to march down to the other side of the floor, stand on a desk, and rip down the scoreboard screens. Wow. Micromanagement? My intention was the exact opposite!

I had given up trying to figure out the tactical solution. I wanted to empower the front-line folks with knowledge and tools to figure out their own solution! Great intentions, but I totally failed on execution. I did not get "buy-in" in advance. A big failure on my part. I didn't know how to lead change.

At the time, we simply were not a change-oriented organization. We didn't know how to get "buy-in," so the imposition of top-down change, the command and control approach, was a total disaster.

Lessons Learned

Well, I learned a lot from that experience and discussed those revelations with just about everyone I knew in the business world. I have since read most of Professor Kotter's books and articles, and now know enough to achieve sufficient buy-in well in advance of implementing anything new. I have concluded that you cannot dictate change through command and control, which is a tough organizational business model.

I do need to mention, however, that the scoreboards did stay up. I did a lot of apologizing and explaining, and in short order folks started to take tactical actions on their own, quickly and dramatically improving our telephone answer rate. Empowered, aligned and engaged, the front-like folks did in several months what senior management couldn't do in 12 years. This is a story I love to tell.

So, while metrics are critical, and everyone needs to get comfortable using metrics for self and team management, be careful. The purpose behind metrics, as I learned, can be misconstrued as micromanagement. You need to teach people the real purpose behind metrics and how to use them. This takes time and work. I encourage you to read *Moneyball: The Art of Winning an Unfair Game,* Jack Stack's *The Great Game of Business* and Professor Kotter's *Leading Change* and *Buy-In.*

Also try to get some thought leaders (influencers) in your company to read these books as well. Metric literacy needs to be explained and taught, but it is well worth the time and investment.

THE IMPACT OF METRIC LITERACY

I firmly believe that every position and tactic needs to have at least one metric (in addition to your quarterly and annual goals), and every meeting should discuss and review metrics. Remember the maxim, "What gets measured, gets done."

Here are a couple of additional observations based on our experience:

I have found that it takes folks time to learn how to use metrics, so have some patience. For a while, people will report too many metrics, then too few. At first, some metrics will be totally irrelevant, others will be marginally relevant and some will mean something. For a while folks reported metrics but did not discuss or analyze their tactical meaning. What I mean by this is that people must ask whether metrics indicate whether your tactical activity is accomplishing the desired outcome. Encourage discussion around the metrics and teach your thought leaders to constantly ask "why?" Make sure that everyone's metrics are the *right* metrics to determine whether you are achieving your desired outcome. Remember, you get what you measure. So, while it does take time to become a metric-literate organization, you can hasten this transformation by encouraging people to drill down on the meaning of each metric. This will lead to some awesome metrics-based discussions.

Metric literacy takes not only time, but experience and coaching. It took us almost a year for folks to become very comfortable and proficient with using metrics. Now, people are very adept at figuring out which metrics really matter. I have gone into meetings, the metrics are up on the screen, and there is an unbelievably insightful discussion around tactics that is grounded in fact. This is a beautiful thing to watch.

Even more beautiful to know is that it is happening all over your company on a daily basis. People are using metrics to make tactical decisions, without consulting senior management. This is an important point. Senior management cannot own or dictate metrics (except for the KPIs tied to the big annual goals).

METRICS AND THE TRIBE

Metrics belong to the tribe. Metric literacy empowers and aligns the tribe. It keeps your goals front and center (is your team winning or losing?) and it allows for tactical confidence. *Hey, let's try this and see if it works. We can course-correct if it isn't working.* We have our metrics. We know what we are doing. Folks are emboldened to take tactical action steps. You also want a lot of metrics sharing and group discussion about them. It needs to become part of your tribal culture.

Which should come first—metric literacy or the systems to collect, analyze and present metrics? This is a good question. We pushed metric literacy ahead of the systems. The systems followed. While this created some frustrations around the time and difficulty in collecting, analyzing and presenting metrics, it then developed the organizational understanding and demand for the appropriate systems. The tribe began to ask for the systems. The need was clearly articulated.

When we started building the systems, the people putting them together partnered with different groups from around the company who had a relatively good understanding of what they wanted and also reacted favorably to many of the ideas presented by the tech folks. We would not have had a good partnership between the tech folks and the operating and service people unless we had achieved a certain level of company-wide metrics literacy first.

I would also add that at this point there is good collaboration around how metrics are presented. This too takes some time and thought but is critical to their successful use. Metrics must be presented in an easy-to-understanding manner—graphs, charts, colors, trend lines, and so on. This is important; it helps folks see and understand what the numbers mean. Metrics are telling us where we have been and where we are going.

The bottom line: Metrics facilitate tactical liberation. Accountability, transparency, self-management. *Are your tactics working? Are they moving you toward your goals?* Metrics enable decision-making based on data rather than on gut, hearsay and anecdote. Operational ownership of metrics helps avoid micromanagement by senior management.

CHAPTER SUMMARY

You cannot step back from micromanaging and expect an aligned, engaged, empowered and on-fire tribe unless you build your Constitutional Framework, instill a disciplined meeting rhythm, and teach metric literacy. You must give folks the skills and tools and the framework to self-execute and to self-manage. This takes a lot of time and leadership.

Main chapter points include:

➤ Metrics help you move toward your BHAG.

➤ Metric literacy empowers employees, enabling you to avoid micromanagement.

➤ Everyone, not just senior management, needs to know what the metric "score" is at all times.

➤ You want total transparency around your goals and your metrics.

➤ Visible metrics focus the whole company on its quarterly and annual goals. Every goal, every project and anything you want to improve should have at least one metric.

➤ Key Performance Indicators (KPIs) are essential, and are tied to your goals.

➤ Metrics enable self-management, providing an objective scoreboard for whether your tactics are working. They rely on data rather than tradition, whim, hearsay or anecdote.

➤ Get serious with metric literacy now, without further delay.

➤ Make sure you have metrics buy-in and ownership from the entire workforce before implementing them.

In upcoming chapters, I discuss the importance of strong tribal culture, an obsession with communication, comfort with change, risk and failure, having the right players who embrace personal growth, and, my newest area of learning, building an organizational culture of physical and mental wellness and wellbeing.

7

Building and Feeding a Tribal Culture

Your Constitutional Framework. A disciplined meeting rhythm. Metric literacy. These all are necessary ingredients for a team that is aligned, engaged and empowered. However, there is more. You also need an intense, positive and unique organizational culture, a vibrant, nurturing identity that fuels the power of these principles.

Here is the definition of culture that we use at Ambrose:

The set of shared attitudes, values, goals and practices that characterize an institution, organization or group.

When you think about all of the key elements that I have discussed so far, it's pretty obvious that they boil down to shared attitudes, values, goals and practices. Buying into these shared values helps create a strong tribal experience. It is the glue. Culture needs to be owned by every tribal member. Each member must feel responsible for shaping, upholding and protecting the company's culture.

ACHIEVING BIG THINGS

Your culture is one of your organization's greatest assets, period. It is built on and around your Constitutional Framework. You must constantly invest in your company culture, building and nourishing the tribe. You must amp it up if you want to achieve big things.

At Ambrose we put an incredible amount of energy, thought, time and money into building and nurturing our tribal culture. We do it because a strong and healthy culture is necessary for the tribe, and our company, to flourish. A vibrant, participatory tribal culture motivates each of us to strive and excel as individuals. It inspires each person to contribute his or her maximum to achieve the tribe's goals. It unites us. We are all codependent on one another and on the tribe for success.

Remember that your BHAG must be so grand that individual heroics are not sufficient to achieve it. A strong tribal, team effort is necessary to reach your goals; otherwise, those goals are simply not ambitious enough.

Duke Basketball coach Mike Krzyzewski described in his fine book, *Leading with the Heart: Coach K's Successful Strategies for Basketball, Business, and Life,* how he constantly reminds his team that the fist is stronger than any one finger. So, again, there's no original thinking here on my part. It takes teamwork to win the championship.

▼ PYRAMID PERSPECTIVE:
Our Enabling Culture

By Stacey Molski, Sales and Marketing
Fellow Ambrosian since April 2010

During my first week at Ambrose, I attended a training session on how best to communicate via email and phone. Immediately after this training, I sighed and thought, "Well, there's just no way *this* is going to work. I just don't talk like that. That's not who I am."

That was more than two and a half years ago. Ambrose doesn't give that training anymore. In fact, I'll bet that nobody even remembers it but me.

That communications training probably wasn't a big deal for most people in the company, but it was for me. It was like a symbol that I, with an arts background, was now in the corporate world, and that this was how you had to talk in the corporate world if you wanted to fit in with everyone else. Well, luckily I didn't have to believe that for very long. Shortly after I started with Ambrose, the company underwent a cultural shift.

I can't speak for Ambrose before the time I started, but from my point of view there has been a huge change in the culture of the company between the time I joined and now. Sure, we're an HR company and we work hard and handle lots of serious matters, but that doesn't mean we can't have fun. I think that everyone realizes this now.

These days I (and most of my coworkers) rarely send an email without including some little thing solely for the purpose of entertaining one another. The point is not that everyone at every company needs to send silly emails. Not at all; you need to do what works for you. The point is that people are not merely *allowed* to be themselves, they are *encouraged*. We have many distinctive individuals at Ambrose, each with unique strengths, weaknesses and personality traits. The crazy thing is that everyone totally supports one another (honestly). Maybe I'm off base, but I think this is fairly unusual in the business world. No one is fighting each other or undermining each other in order to get ahead. They all just want to come together and do the best they can so that they, and the company, can grow.

I am always taken aback by the support and encouragement I receive when I take on projects, especially ones that are a real challenge for me. There have been times when I've sat there saying, "I don't know about this, guys…" and instead of the team saying " Yeah, we should just let so-and-so do it," I have a room full of excited people telling me that whatever I'm doing is going be so awesome and they can't wait to see it. And they *really mean it*.

For me, it is a real privilege to work in an environment like this with people whom I truly consider to be my friends. I think this is a sentiment most people at Ambrose share. I know for a fact that the sheer number of opportunities I have had at Ambrose is tenfold compared to what I'd get to do at another company. It's easy to grow when you work with people who want you to thrive. It's also a lot easier to work late on those tough projects when the people with whom you work know how to make you laugh. Yes, we do a lot of work. But we have a whole lot of fun.

PROTECTING STAKEHOLDERS

If you are an investor or large shareholder in a company, you have yet another reason why you should spend some time focusing on the strength and health of its culture. That's because a strong culture can prevent bad things from happening.

When you have a healthy and growing tribal culture that is stronger than any one ego, stronger than the CEO's ego or the founder's ego, then its benefits will extend far beyond employee performance to protect all of your organization's *stakeholders:* shareholders, employees, vendors, customers, the government and the community. After all, as the "heart and soul" of the organization, your culture protects the company and all of its stakeholders from malfeasant individuals, rogue leadership and bad "group think." This is important stuff that most entrepreneurs underestimate.

A strong tribal culture acts as an alter ego to the individual ego. It keeps us all in check, and keeps any one individual, particularly in leadership, from "taking the company rogue." Unfortunately, there are plenty of sad examples elsewhere where a malfeasant CEO ran roughshod over a complacent, weak or unhealthy culture, and I discuss one such case later in this chapter.

Overall, the tribe and its culture, the collective, are more important than any one individual. The team is more important than any one player, no matter how good he or she is. For this reason, I view a strong, healthy culture as a protector of my equity investment in Ambrose.

WE ARE ALL TRIBAL ANIMALS

There is another reason why you need to build a strong, healthy culture: We are tribal animals; communal people. This is human nature.

A strong, healthy culture gives us a sense of purpose and of belonging. Simply, it's fun. We crave it. Most people love being on a team, especially a highly functional, supportive, winning team. You must deliver to your people that strong tribal cultural experience. As a leader, this is a big part of your job. If you are stuck in the tactical day-to-day, you will not have the time and the clarity to focus on building and sustaining your company's culture. As a leader, you need to realize that it isn't about you. It isn't about your ego. It's about everyone else and their ego. You want everyone in your company to get to the top of Maslow's hierarchy of needs—self-actualization. This is leadership.

People want a positive tribal, team experience. I was reminded of this recently when I attended a corporate wellness conference in San Diego. At the Hyatt, there was another conference, the west coast leadership of Harley-Davidson Owner Groups (HOGs). These clubs are intensely tribal. They are cult-like.

Now think about this: Harley-Davison has tribal customers. Wow. This is your goal as a leader. Turn your company, and then your customers, into a tribal cult.

Most of us will never get to the Harley-Davidson level, but if you can get halfway there, I would consider that a success. When you have a very strong company culture, your customers will feel it. You want to start internally with a very strong company culture and then let it radiate out to your customers. People enjoy a great, genuine tribal experience, especially when they own it and are responsible for protecting it.

ACTIVELY DEFINING YOUR CULTURE

Okay, so craving a strong, positive tribal culture is human nature. Fair enough, but now consider this: *You can't be passive about your culture.* It will not happen on its own. You have to actively define it. Its foundation is your Constitutional Framework, core values and BHAG.

You must actively develop your culture and, most importantly, constantly reinforce it. You are never, ever done strengthening your culture. What happens if you don't take ownership and control of your culture? It's going to devolve in a way that you're not going to like.

Read the classic *Lord of the Flies* by William Golding. A group of British schoolchildren is marooned on an island, removed from their social structure, and what happens? They tribally devolve toward a very ugly place. They culturally run amuck. Who has worked or been in an environment where the culture devolved to an ugly, nasty place? Most of us.

Have you ever worked at a law firm? I have. Most law firms are culturally adrift (I am being nice), with low morale. You definitely do not want this to happen to your company. Do not ignore your culture. Otherwise, you risk having bad things happen. You surely will not get the best out of folks. It will not inspire. Your great human capital will opt out and depart. You want everyone to feel great every day. That is your goal as a leader.

Leadership must put a lot of time and energy into developing, building and strengthening a positive company culture. This takes a lot of work, but it cannot be ignored. As a leader, you should worry about your culture every day and night. You should think constantly about ways to strengthen your company culture. This is not goofy, soft stuff. This is real. Your human capital demands and expects this, especially in a world where there are choices.

There are some great books on this topic, including *Tribal Leadership* by Dave Logan, John King, and Halee Fischer-Wright, *Delivering Happiness: A Path to Profits, Passion, and Purpose* by Tony Hsieh and Seth Godin's *Tribes: We Need You to Lead Us*. If you read these books, you'll expand your insight on the many shades of organizational tribal culture.

You need to push yourself into an uncomfortable zone and stay there. If you think you are being too "touchy-feely" on the culture front, then good. Keep it up.

SOURCING CULTURAL LEADERS

Central to building and maintaining a strong tribal culture are tribal leaders. They're indispensable. So, who are your cultural leaders? This is something you need to spend time thinking about, and it has nothing to do with the organizational chart.

You already have people in your organization who are cultural leaders, people who clearly embody your company's core values, so you need to consciously identify them, hold them up as examples, praise them and shine a light on them. You also need to make a concerted, methodical effort to hire the right people for an ideal cultural fit—individuals who embody your company's values in everything they do, and who will be instrumental in moving your business forward. Then you need to love, embrace, and encourage all of these people. They must be involved in the ongoing hiring process. They need to be developed and promoted. These are very important people to your organization.

How do you identify cultural leaders you may already have? First, leadership must be vocal in letting everyone know that culture and cultural leaders are important and highly regarded members of the community. I recommend that you also have a voluntary cultural committee with a budget. This committee cannot be controlled or managed by leadership. Cultural leaders will self identify, volunteer and put on great tribe building events (Side note: We do require the cultural committee to report its event metrics to the whole company, including attendance, "customer" satisfaction, and so on).

When you hire, you must interview for cultural fit. How you do that? Well, here are three ways to begin:

> Your culture must be apparent on your company website. For example, our site displays our core values and our Constitutional Framework, as well as a video about our people and our culture. (Additionally, I have blogged extensively on this topic and have now written this book.)

> When candidates come in for an interview, they must sit down with folks outside of the department that they are looking to join. This is so that colleagues outside of the hiring department can interview the candidate solely for cultural fit.

> Your interview assessment and evaluation processes must specifically and extensively address culture and core value alignment. This must become part of the hiring discussions with the candidate and internally when evaluating that person. You must have this conversation with the candidate. Interviewers must explore the candidate's core value fit with the company.

Every candidate needs to fully understand your culture, have the opportunity to ask as many questions as necessary and also understand how important culture is to your organization. Both the company and the candidate must come to the agreement that a cultural fit exists before you hire. You want each candidate to understand up front the responsibilities associated with joining your community.

Culture and core values are an important part of the hiring process. You want your culture to be so apparent that candidates are intentionally opting into it. You want to recruit folks who want to join your tribe.

Throughout our hiring, evaluation and coaching process—as well as during our employee-of-the-quarter nominating process—we specifically and extensively address culture. We have discussions about who is "culturally strong," and this is an important factor in all of our hiring and promoting decisions.

Sourcing tribal leaders is a continuous process critical to the success of your organization.

SOURCING TRIBAL LEADERS

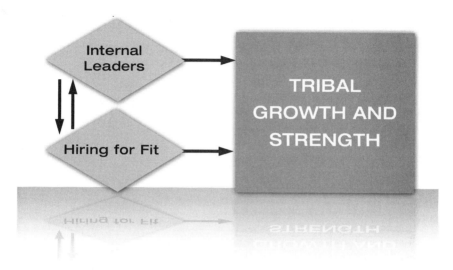

Sourcing tribal leaders is a continuous process critical to the success of your organization.

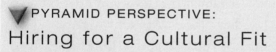

▼ PYRAMID PERSPECTIVE:

Hiring for a Cultural Fit

By Christopher Gaine, Sales
Fellow Ambrosian since March 2012

Assuring that Ambrose remains a special place starts with the hiring process. Not only is it vertical in terms of being a multistep process where you meet with people at different levels of the company, but it also contains great breadth; the process looks at you from many angles, with a special emphasis on whether you meet Ambrose's six core values.

Dedication, Integrity, Excellence, to Teach and to be Taught, Humility and Respect are Ambrose's lifeblood. As an employee or prospective employee, you are expected to adhere to or are measured against these values. During my initial interview, I was oblivious to these specifics, but became keenly aware that I was being evaluated on more than just my technical skills or business accomplishments.

The second round of interviews was not unlike the first, but this time I met with people who were to be my peers. What struck me at this point was not the questions but the fact that *everyone* with whom I spoke seemed to be very happy. How was this possible? A Wall Street interview typically is a contest of intelligence where the hiring manager basically asks you a series of questions, lasting to the point at which that person eventually stumps you or you both declare a sort of truce after discovering that you have a friend in common somewhere. That friend then reaches out on your behalf and the deal is sealed.

My Ambrose interview was not that way at all. Instead, I found myself fielding questions that related to the company's core values. A questioner would ask, "Tell me about a great accomplishment" and then would listen for signs of humility. Or, someone would ask me how I would handle a troubling situation, then would listen intently to see if I was respectful to others' opinions or whether I came off as a know-it-all.

Ambrose believes that if you can meet its core values, then that is the most important thing, and you can be taught a skill in order to fit in somewhere and flourish. If you are the best in the world in that skill but can't address your peers in a respectful manner and understand that even you can be taught something, then you are not who they want on their team because the chemistry will be destroyed. After seeing this in action now for several months, I am a huge believer in the Ambrose way.

My third round in the interview process consisted of an in-depth personality and aptitude test, which then opened the door for the fourth round, the most different interviewing session I have ever had. Referred to as "Topgrading," it consists of one person asking you questions involving topics going back as far as high school while another for the most part is a passive observer. The entire process can take several hours and is extremely thorough.

The reference stage comes last, where your colleagues and friends are put through a condensed version of stages one through four. I have never been through something like this before in my life!

RUNNING A CULTURE CLASS

Every new hire at Ambrose must go through a cultural orientation class. This class should be taught by a company leader, should be given as soon as possible after the hire date and is absolutely mandatory for all new hires. All new hires are also required to read my blog (and now, this book), although I have found that most read it before they even interview at Ambrose. This helps them gain an understanding of our history, who we are, how we operate, what is important to us and what is expected from each Ambrosian.

My cultural class is two and a half hours and is titled "Alignment." That's basically it. I cover all of the material that appears in my blog postings and in this book. This orientation encompasses our Constitutional Framework, the disciplined meeting rhythm, metric literacy, the importance of culture and tribalism, communication, change, risk and failure and embracing personal growth. Yes, I have it all in a PowerPoint deck. I love teaching this class, and there are very few excuses available to someone to miss it. "I am too busy" is not one of them.

This class is one of the most critical components of my job. When leadership teaches this class to all new hires, you are also sending a very powerful message to everyone about how important these things are to individual and collective success. I also clearly communicate to all new hires that this is the social compact we have entered into. This is the agreement we are all making at Ambrose with each other and this is what allows us to avoid micromanagement and allow for self-actualization in an aligned manner. Freedom, so to speak, has responsibilities.

Dov Frohman writes about formal cultural orientation in his book *Leadership the Hard Way.* Again, this stuff just doesn't happen on its own. You must take an active role in developing a strong, positive tribal culture. A formal cultural orientation for all new hires is an absolute necessity. They have to understand the culture before they can become cultural participants, leaders and guardians. They also need to understand your Constitutional Framework and the social compact before they can get out on the field and play the game.

NURTURING THE TRIBE THROUGH CULTURAL EVENTS AND RECOGNITION

You cannot build a strong, healthy culture by yourself. You need everyone in the entire company to feel fully liberated to join in this tribe-building endeavor. Everyone needs to know that leadership places a very high value on your culture and tribalism. This means that you must implement and follow a continual program of cultural events and recognition.

Cultural leaders and guardians are your cheerleaders for this task. You had cheerleaders in your high school, and now you need to find these people in your company, and then celebrate, liberate and empower them to help build and nurture the tribe. These leaders must be involved in the cultural event planning process.

You need to talk about your culture all the time. You need to get the tribe and its cultural leaders going in the right direction. Cultural events help you do this, because they make sure everyone knows that leadership places a paramount importance on your culture.

Shout-Outs, Storytelling and Other Recognitions

Constant engagement and celebration, a lot of celebration at your meetings and plenty of shout-outs, particularly around core values, annual and quarterly goals and BHAG. These are things we encourage constantly, and especially at every quarterly meeting. Employee recognition should be constant and ongoing, including "Employees of the Month" and "Employees of the Quarter" honors.

At Ambrose, we also have shout-outs in the dailies that cascade up through the organization. We even have what we call *fish bowl shout-outs,* and here's how they work: When someone does something great, you write it up and drop it in a fish bowl. Once a month, folks are selected from the fishbowl, celebrated at the monthly meeting and treated to a nice celebratory lunch.

Another way to celebrate your tribal members and their achievements is through constant storytelling. Before each quarterly meeting and annual holiday party, I solicit and receive dozens of stories from folks throughout the company about their peers living our core values, showing leadership and achieving things that move us toward our goals. Then, in front of the whole company, I talk about our culture, our core values, and our goals, reading two dozen or so stories about our awesome people.

After each shout-out, the tribe goes wild. (Distribute noisemakers in advance.) Everyone feels great. This quarterly task is my personal favorite, and one of the most important parts of my job at Ambrose (along with teaching my alignment class). Tribe-building through stories. Again, nothing new here (think Homer's *Iliad* and the *Odyssey*).

EXPANDING YOUR TRIBE

As you grow, as you hire new employees, as you expand geographically, as time goes by, forces will conspire to pull your culture apart, so you must constantly invest in, define, develop, evolve and reinforce your tribe.

When you expand geographically, you need a *Chef du Cite* (a Club Med term)—someone who is responsible for the culture at the new geographic location. In our constant effort to focus on ways to strengthen and improve the health of our culture, we recently started an annual conference called AmbroseConnects for our stakeholders: our employees, clients, trusted advisors, prospects and vendors. It is basically a giant, annual tribal gathering.

AmbroseConnects

Our most recent AmbroseConnects event brought together more than 200 decision-makers from more than 100 forward-thinking small businesses, along with most of our employees from around the country. In the spirit of one of Ambrose's core values, "To Teach and to be Taught," the full-day agenda featured Ambrose's best-practices thought leadership content, but also included outside experts in financial services, business and two members of the U.S. Congress leading a variety of panels and seminars. Dr. Paul Marciano, author of the book *Carrots and Sticks Won't Work* and a leading authority on employee engagement and retention, presented the opening keynote. This annual tribal gathering is a powerful and engaging cultural and learning experience for everyone who attends.

As we have grown and expanded, we have felt the need for additional "tools" to strengthen our tribal culture. This event and even planning for it has a huge impact on strengthening our tribal culture and expanding it to embrace our vendors, clients and trusted advisors. We are constantly thinking of and experimenting with other ideas to strengthen our tribal culture.

WHEN CULTURE IS A CULT

I look at this tribal culture as cult-like, but I understand that such a characterization carries some baggage. After all, the world is full of kooky cults, and some of them are way out there.

Culture, cult—same word. Yes, some of those cults are in the "danger zone," but the vast majority of workplaces are very, very far, too far, from that sort of cult status. You have a long way to go before you have to worry, so ramp it up. Your quarterly and monthly meetings need to be a tribal experience. Use culture in your hiring process. Tell a lot of stories. Talk about your culture all the time, host an annual "tribal" conference such as AmbroseConnects and keep those employee shout-outs and recognition awards coming.

Don't be nervous about going down this road. Ask yourself, are you a cultural leader? You need to be one and you need to find fellow compatriots. This is a necessary component of building an aligned, engaged, empowered and on-fire organization.

CULTURAL MISMATCH: A SHORT STORY

A number of years ago, we were beginning to strengthen our culture, but it wasn't strong enough. We had hired and promoted a very bright, technically competent fellow to a very senior management position. A large portion of the company reported to this individual. A number of us were beginning to take the company in the new direction that I have described in this book. We had been getting folks throughout the company to attend conferences and read many of the books I have referenced. I was holding lunches regularly with these people to discuss all of my ideas. Everyone was excited.

While all of this was going on this senior leader told me what I wanted to hear. However, behind my back he told others that he thought all of the above was foolishness. Out of sight, he ruled with an iron fist—total command and control, intense micromanagement, intimidation, fear, belittlement. People were getting one message from the company's tribal leaders, but "on the ground," in their everyday jobs, they were experiencing something totally different.

Because our culture was not as strong as it needed to be, it took us too long to identify and eject this person. This fellow did significant damage while he was around. People quit and morale was very low. He didn't come close to getting the most out of people. In fact, the opposite was true. He *diminished* people. Employees felt terrible about themselves. If they didn't quit, they disengaged. This is not good.

I take full responsibility for this failure. If we had a stronger, more intense and vibrant tribal culture at the time, then that more confident, cohesive tribe would have more quickly invoked our core values to eject this fellow as a cultural mismatch. Your core values, and your culture, need to be so strong that they can quickly identify and eject an ill-fitting senior manager.

While you need a Constitutional Framework, a disciplined meeting rhythm and metric literacy, a strong tribal culture really is the glue that holds the whole thing together. It brings everything to life. This is how you get the best out of every person at your company in an aligned, engaged and empowered way. This is strategic leadership.

CHAPTER SUMMARY

How strong is your culture? In this chapter I discussed the importance of building a strong organizational culture—a tribe. You can define a culture or tribe as "the set of shared attitudes, values, goals, and practices that characterizes an institution, organization or group."

Main chapter points include:

➤ A strong tribal culture is necessary to achieve big things—goals that no individual alone can reach—so you must nurture a strong culture. It's probably the most important thing you will do as a leader.

➤ Tribalism includes "buy-in" to all of your core values.

➤ A strong, effective tribe includes hiring for a cultural fit.

➤ Constant engagement and recognition through cultural events is a key component for supporting and growing your tribal culture.

➤ When tribalism is strong, it encompasses all stakeholders—even your customers.

➤ Cultural leaders are everywhere in your organization, but you must identify them, and then empower them to help build and nourish the tribe.

➤ Is your tribe strong enough? If it is, it will help identify and eject those who would otherwise diminish employees and hold back your success.

➤ A strong culture is a "cult," but not in a bad way!

In the next chapter I discuss a few additional and necessary ingredients: an obsession with communication; comfort with change, risk and failure; having the right players who embrace personal growth; and, my newest area of learning, building an organizational culture of physical and mental wellness and wellbeing (a topic that I believe is very closely tied to building a strong, tribal culture). At Ambrose, this is how we have built an aligned, empowered, engaged and on-fire tribe.

8 Communicate, Communicate, Communicate

For years, we at Ambrose were pathetically weak communicators. By the time we had grown to 35 people, our employees had not only disconnected from leadership, but also from one another. Information wasn't flowing from our front-line people through the company to other employees and to leadership.

We were unable to agree on goals because we depended on anecdotes and half-truths. Conversely, our strategic vision, which was flawed at the time because leadership didn't have enough information, was not communicated back through the company. It also was very difficult to make strategic decisions because we didn't have the facts.

Strategic vision, facts, data and information simply did not religiously pulse through our company. Worse, some people had more information than others, and some just had the wrong information. It was hard to tell fact from fiction. This created an incredible amount of dysfunction and argument. We were not a participatory tribal team on any level. We were misaligned with each other and with our customers.

Once you become metric-literate and support a constant flow of good information—annual and quarterly goals, BHAG, key performance indicators (KPIs), core values, initiatives, stories, achievements, and failures, and particularly what you learned from those failures—to pulse through your company on a daily basis, it becomes much easier to then focus on goals, priorities and solutions as a tribe. You move past arguing over the facts and put your individual and collective energy into focusing on strategic goals, priorities and tactical solutions. You are now also capable of bringing in a much larger group of participants because more folks are armed with information. You cannot ask, and expect, people to participate in the great game of business unless they have the facts and know the goals.

First, everyone needs to be in the know and then everyone must be asked to participate. This is where you must lead your company. As a leader, my goal is for everyone to know *more* than me so that they can contribute in a truly meaningful way. Organizationally you must have zero tolerance for information hoarders, particularly when this is done for individualistic ego purposes—that is, to make the hoarder look smarter than others. This pathetic old trick must be relegated to the trash heap.

It boils down to this: You cannot underestimate the importance of the constant flow of good information and ideas. You must have a culture that obsesses about communicating information, ideas, goals, priorities, problems and solutions. This must become a company-wide cultural obsession. Sharing good information must become your cultural norm.

GOSSIP IS GOOD

I read a great short article in the September 2010 issue of the *Harvard Business Review*, written by Professor Joe Labianca. It was "It's Not 'Unprofessional' to Gossip at Work," and it made a lot of sense to me. You cannot stop "water cooler gossip," so don't waste your time trying. On the contrary, embrace it. Gossip is human nature. Gossip is good. It is tribal.

We all love to gossip and it is socially bonding. It connects us. It is anti-hierarchical. You want a lot of informal, nonhierarchical chatter. Here is the important point though: You need enough good information flowing through your company so that the "gossip" is based in truths and facts. If everyone knows your goals, your core purpose, brand promise, core values and knows the score (metrics), then water-cooler chatter will be based on truth and facts and not on half-truths, innuendo and misinformation. This is how you deal with gossip: Keep your company full of the truth.

That disciplined meeting rhythm is the main nervous system through which you keep your company full of truths and facts. Quality communication is transported in large part by a strong, functional meeting rhythm. You also want a lot of knowledgeable, tribal, informal water-cooler chit-chat. This is good—it gets everyone's left brain (rote) and right brain (creative) working. Misstatements of facts and truths will be exposed and corrected, and tactical problems will be solved. This sort of "good gossip" shows that people are engaged. This truly is a good thing.

THE DAILY 'BROSE AND COLLABORATIVE SOCIAL MEDIA

Intense, constant communication at Ambrose also is spread via an internal blog called *The Daily 'Brose*, the content of which is guided by our six core values (Humility, Integrity, Respect, Excellence, Dedication and to Teach and to be Taught). Anyone can post and add comments on *The Daily 'Brose*.

Many folks have posted a variety of messages on *The Daily 'Brose*. It is, and must be, a comfortable place (just like your meetings). It includes postings on product launches, all sorts of achievements, job openings, metrics, goals, thoughts about interesting articles, books and videos and shout-outs. It also includes plenty of postings totally unrelated to our business, such as, for example, photos from the last big snow storm, a video of Thierry Henry's first goal for the New York Red Bulls, and much more.

Following are some recent postings from *The Daily 'Brose*. All new hires also post "Hellos" telling us about themselves and their interests. Many people post about new family additions and other cool and exciting things in their lives.

THE DAILY 'BROSE
Hurricane Sandy: How to Help

Hello all!

ACCA mentioned wanting to create a digital resource for how to help those affected by Hurricane Sandy. I got us started with a catch-all sort of document.

I've put in the Nose (thanks for the training today, JBray!)

The document includes tips on donating and volunteering, as well as links to all sorts of sites that can give you more information. We'd love for this to stay up-to-date, so if you hear of any opportunities or have any ideas on how to help, please add them to the comments in the Nose.

I am sharing this here in case you don't see it in the Nose activity, but we'd like to keep all of the information in the Nose, so please, if you have comments, post them in the Nose, not here.

Thanks!

If there's something strange in our neighborhood...who ya gonna call? HR Services!

Last night, HR Services celebrated meeting our quarterly goals with a ghost tour of the Financial District. As you can see from the photo (bright spots in the right corner of the page), we spotted many ghostly specters. Through the evening mist, our tour guide took us through dark and narrow streets, ensuring we were well protected with stereo equipment and headsets. We walked carefully, making sure neither a pedestrian nor an Occupy Wall Streeter hosing down the street would stop us from reaching our Stone Street destination. As you may already know, HR Services ain't afraid o' no ghost!

Crains Fast 50: Ambrose is 32 out of 50

Good morning Team Ambrose,

AmbroseMania is running wild. If you want a piece of this, get on the A-train!!!!!!

In Crain's first-ever Fast 50 NY fastest-growing small to medium size businesses, we placed an impressive 32nd out of 50. This is super exciting and it really is because we have the best human capital across many industries. I can't say it enough. We have set high expectations here and we continually break through new grounds and barriers everyday in everything that we do. Simply amazing and we all should be proud of this accomplishment.

Many thanks to those who were "responsible" for moving this initiative forward. You know who you are, Internal Director of HR. And I'm sure I'm forgetting others.

So to all, to summarize, **"This is Ambrose: Where People Count!!!!!!!!!!!!"**

Again, Congratulations guys!!!! The fun has just begun.

The Daily 'Brose allows for anyone to easily communicate to the tribe. When I travel away from the office, *The Daily 'Brose* keeps me connected with the tribe. I have heard the same report from folks in our other geographically dispersed offices, from folks who work from home, and particularly from the folks on family leave.

Honestly, when we launched *The Daily 'Brose* we had not thought of the folks on family leave, but I cannot say how excited I was when they returned to work and immediately commented on how the blog had helped them stay connected with their extended Ambrose family—their tribe. That is neat. The disciplined meeting rhythm, metric literacy, and our internal blog are just three internal processes that we use to flow a lot of good, accurate information through the company so we can stay tribally engaged with one another.

▼ PYRAMID PERSPECTIVE:
Publishing *The Daily 'Brose*

By Lee Schatzberg, Client Services
Fellow Ambrosian since July 2010

I started at Ambrose a month after graduating college, excited and eager to learn, but not sure what to expect from the corporate world (or "real life" as I referred to it while still in school). My first day was what I would imagine most people's first day at work to be—a little (okay, *extremely*) nerve-wracking as I tried desperately to remember who everyone was and gain a better understanding of how things worked at Ambrose. I had so many questions. How do departments interact? How formal do my emails need to be? Do people go out for lunch or bring their own? Ambrose employed only around 80 people at the time, but it seemed huge to me.

Also new to Ambrose was our internal blog, *The Daily 'Brose*. I received an email on my first day from a member of our marketing team with instructions for setting up a personal WordPress account that would let me post on the blog. With a little extra time on my hands as I settled in to the new position, I logged in to check it out. I was intrigued but admittedly also a bit skeptical. The blog was only seven days old and there were fewer than 10 posts—not a lot of substance. It seemed that after my first day, however, everyone at Ambrose took the blog idea and ran with it.

The number of blog posts each day began multiplying rapidly, and it became clear to me pretty quickly that I somehow needed to make my *Daily 'Brose* debut. By posting, I would essentially be declaring, "I work here now and I am going to make a positive impact on this company!" I took the plunge by posting a picture of myself and several other new employees on the company's annual boat cruise, which occurred about two weeks after I started. After proofreading my photo caption at least three times, I took a deep breath and with one click sent my contribution out into cyberspace. I wondered nervously what people would think of my post, and to my surprise I received two comments within minutes. "Great pic!" said our director of 401(k), who worked in a different office and had not yet met me. I immediately felt welcomed.

After that first month, *The Daily 'Brose* flourished and became a forum for almost anything Ambrose-related. It became a place for us to proudly post news articles about our clients, pictures of new babies and other milestones, and recognition for one another. We use it to learn about each other and discover what makes everyone tick. It's where I discovered that a member of our tech team spends his vacations building homes for underprivileged families, and that our office manager was completely hilarious.

To this day, few things are more satisfying at work than getting a comment on a blog post, be it from the person sitting next to you or one of our CEOs. The blog has continued to develop and has come to represent all of our personalities both inside and outside of Ambrose. As our company grows, the blog plays a key role in maintaining a tight-knit environment.

The key to *The Daily 'Brose's* success was, and continues to be, our employees. Our pervasive and open company culture is what encourages people to share what they have to say on the *'Brose,* and in turn the blog represents and fosters our company culture. I'm glad I recognized early on that this blog was going to be *big*, but now, when new employees start, we waste no time telling them to get on there to introduce themselves to the rest of the company. Now everyone gets a little extra nudge to log in and announce, "I'm here, I'm excited and I'm going to make a valuable contribution to the Ambrose community."

Ambrose has also recently embraced several really exciting collaborative social media platforms that have facilitated some incredible geographically liberating collaboration, transparency and sharing of information and ideas. The adoption of these products came from the "front lines" and has taken off like wildfire. They've taken alignment, empowerment and engagement to a whole new level.

COMMUNICATIONS COACHING

Like anything else, people have varying levels of skill when it comes to communicating, and everyone can get better, especially when it comes to making presentations. Coach Leonard Peters is a talented theater professional we've hired to run workshops internally at Ambrose to develop people's presentation skills (mine included). We want our employees to be both excellent and *comfortable* communicators, whether they're interfacing with colleagues, clients or vendors.

Everyone enjoys Leonard, and his workshops are well attended and effective. Coach Leonard gives people the skills to play a better game. In my opinion, this has been one of our smartest investments in our human capital, and I encourage you to give communications and presentation coaching and training serious consideration in your own organization. Give your people the skills and the opportunities that maximize their potential to participate effectively in the game of business.

As I said, *everyone* can improve his or her communication skills. The presenters, and especially the presentees, will thank you.

REPEAT YOURSELF!

To really drive points home you need to say important things at least three times and in three different ways.

"I sent the email. I sent the memo."

This does not work. People are busy. Your organization is a competitive marketplace. There is a lot going on, with a lot of noise. That is a good thing, but it also means that for important issues folks need to repeat them a lot.

An issue that I wanted Ambrose to focus on recently was wellness. I knew that a dictatorial wellness memo from me wasn't going to achieve a darn thing. So, to raise the importance of this issue, I simply set out on a multifaceted communication initiative. I spoke about wellness at our quarterly meetings, I posted interesting wellness articles on *The Daily 'Brose*, I wrote a blog posting on it, and I sent around a lot of articles and books on the topic to various thought leaders in the company. When thought leaders then started posting wellness articles on *The Daily 'Brose,* I immediately commented positively on those articles and also publicly encouraged their company-wide wellness initiatives.

As I mentioned earlier, we are working on deploying metric scoreboards around the company so that everyone can be fully engaged in the "game" by easily looking up from the "play" to see the current score. This is another form of repetition, and just one more approach to continuously pumping the company full of truths and facts.

I spend a lot of time worrying about the ongoing communication of our Constitutional Framework: core values, BHAG, annual and quarterly goals, core purpose and brand promise. You have to get into this zone. Employees have to look at you and know what you are going to talk about. It never ends. Repeat the important stuff often.

There must be constant communication about progress, or lack thereof, toward the company's quarterly and annual goals. This habit paves the way for tactical innovation and change, minimizes surprises and prevents fear, uncertainty and doubt.

▼ PYRAMID PERSPECTIVE:

Eliminating Fear, Uncertainty and Doubt

By Maya Cohen, Sales
Fellow Ambrosian since 2005

I have been at Ambrose for the past seven years, and during this time I have seen the company undergo a significant transformation. The bulk of this change has been in the last two to three years, with my own perspective driven by the fact that I have been on maternity leave twice during approximately the same period, first with my three-year old son and again with my eight-month-old daughter.

For those who have never experienced being away for 12 whole weeks from a job that they love and are very committed to, I can vouch for the fact that it is bittersweet. It is nice to have some distance from work to spend time with your precious new baby. But this time away is also scary because of the uncertainty about what returning to work will be like, and not knowing what transpired while you were gone.

While I was excited to return to work after my first leave, I had been largely disconnected from my colleagues and from the day-to-office happenings. Four new members had been added to my team. I knew their names, but knew very little about their backgrounds and who they were, and I was scared of having been replaced or forgotten. These days at Ambrose, we often speak about the importance of eliminating fear, uncertainty and doubt (known as FUD). At that time, however, I was filled with FUD and didn't know what to expect when walking through those doors on day one.

Fast-forward three years. My next maternity leave was completely different. Over this short period, Ambrose became culture-obsessed with communication. Communication in every form now pervades our company and we are constantly in touch with our peers, managers and colleagues from other departments through *The Daily 'Brose,* our company blog.

It is amazing that such a simple communicative tool could make such an impact. I came back to work feeling connected to everything that had taken place over 12 weeks, whether it was wellness initiatives, the names and stories of each new hire (and there were many), company-wide metrics and things we like to categorize as "cools."

Aside from keeping employees in multiple offices connected to one another and to Ambrose, the blog has also served as a place where people can be themselves: silly, serious, whatever they fancy. From random posts about the food trucks in our area on a given day, to outreach about charity work that our colleagues are involved with, it is a great way to let people know who you are and what you are interested in without having to send around a company-wide email (something I have never liked doing!). There is only one rule to abide by when posting on *The Daily 'Brose,* and that is abiding by our six core values.

The combination of communicating regularly with internal HR, my manager and the mere existence of a company blog helped to eliminate FUD from my second time on maternity leave. Communication is now an integral part of our culture and it is rampant. *The Daily 'Brose* is one small example of how something simple and easy to use can go a long way, sending ripples of confidence and clarity company-wide.

TACTICAL INNOVATION AND CHANGE

The more information you have flowing through your company, the more tactical experimentation, correction, innovation and change will occur. Everybody must understand where you are, where you are going and whether and why you need to try different tactics. You want total transparency and total understanding. Everyone needs to be fully equipped to solve the company's challenges—you cannot ask this of folks if they don't have a lot of good information. Everyone needs to know as much as or more than leadership.

So, pump the place full of great information and tactically liberate your people. One of the aims of leadership is for everyone to know the company's goals cold and to have the same information as leadership. Conversely, leadership needs to have the same information as employees. You want to create a level playing field among all players regarding goals and key metrics. You cannot work from separate or incomplete data sets.

How can we ask folks to be engaged players in the game of business if they don't know the goals and the score? You can't. How can leadership set strategic goals if they don't have critical data? Everyone must be in the know to self-actualize and to contribute in a meaningful way.

Insecure leaders and managers love to make their peers and their employees feel diminished and inferior. They hoard facts and information and use it to look "smarter" than everyone else (more about the "smartest person in the room" syndrome later). This age-old egocentric tactic makes others feel dumb. This is not good. You must avoid this at all costs. Fire these people immediately. You want *everyone* to contribute their maximum abilities to the cause, so as a leader you need to make sure everyone knows the facts. This encompasses the Constitutional Framework, key metrics and total transparency around issues presented for discussion and solution. How can you have participation and collaboration without a commitment to transparency and openness? This is a huge part of leadership's responsibility and is a prerequisite for getting the best out of everyone.

Remember, as a leader, a big part of your job is to deliver an awesome, tribally participatory experience to each and every individual on your team. So forget about your ego. Focus on everyone else's ego. You want everyone to feel smart. It isn't about you; it's about everyone else. Give them the knowledge to contribute and to succeed—to self-actualize (the top of Maslow's hierarchy of needs). People want to contribute and have a positive impact on moving your company toward its goals. This makes people feel great, so give them that experience.

REAL LEADERS LISTEN MORE

Employees must contribute ideas and solutions. You want them to participate. And, you want leadership to listen more. These two principles are related. Listening—*really* listening—is extremely difficult for most leaders and, based on my experience, the majority are incapable of checking their egos to let others speak and contribute in a meaningful way. (Or, at least they are afraid to give employees the information they need to contribute in a meaningful way).

The traditional organizational chart is misleading, dangerously deceptive and very diminishing. The org chart tells people at the top that they know all the facts and have all the solutions. All right-brain creativity is vested in the folks at the top of the org chart. They espouse while everyone else listens and executes. That is what the org chart says and that is what many people are taught. So folks at the bottom of the traditional org chart are conditioned not to use the creative side of their brain. They are conditioned not to contribute solutions. This makes no sense. You want everyone contributing solutions.

Leaders need to stop crowding out other participants. They must also break the codependency that these other participants have on leaders. Leaders need to learn to move away from the head of the conference room table (I rarely sit at a conference room table but usually against the wall on the side of the room. If I do sit at the table, it is never at the head.) This takes a lot of discipline on the part of leadership.

I challenge you to lead from the back of the boat (or from the side of the court or field; choose your own metaphor). Don't crowd out folks. Pump folks full of good information and then stand on the sidelines and coach. Leaders are coaches, not players. Let others play the game. This isn't easy for most founders, entrepreneurs and leaders. They think they are the star player. You are not. You need to become a coach. Leaders need to listen more.

ENGAGED EMPLOYEES TALK MORE

With leaders on the sidelines, there is more room for employees to talk, discuss, solve and contribute. There is room for them to play the game. You *want* employees who *want* to play the game. However, unless employees are armed with a lot of information—unless they know your Constitutional Framework cold—they will be unable to participate in a way that contributes to the score. They will play poorly and lose. (Insecure leaders love when this happens, but, in fact, it is a leadership failure.) For employees to successfully take the field and play the game of business, you must have an organization obsessed with communicating.

When a level playing field exists for information and progress toward goals, employees will step onto the field, get comfortable and confident with their skills and ideas and play their best. This takes time and constant encouragement from leadership. This needs to become part of your culture, and should be an important personal goal as a leader—as a coach.

By virtue of your position as a leader in the org chart, you have the capability to intimidate and close people down inadvertently. Leaders must be very self-aware of their potentially diminishing effect on people. You must constantly take actions to counteract this effect, such as sitting to the side of the conference room table or against the conference room wall, biting your tongue a lot, publicly praising good ideas, encouraging others and speaking positively. Command and control, conversely, inhibits the free flow of ideas and solutions. Command and control will instill fear and close people down.

One of your goals as a leader is diametrically opposed to command and control: it is to get the best out of each individual and for each individual to have an excellent, successful experience at your company—to be a contributing player. You work for your players and your players work for your fans, your customers.

BUILDING TRUST

Trust is also critical when it comes to comfortable, thoughtful discussion between management and employees and among one another. This is a partnership, and besides pumping people full of knowledge, you need to proactively build a culture of trust, one that has eliminated the fear of retribution.

You cannot have fear of ridicule. People cannot be afraid to say something that may be wrong. You cannot have a culture where it is permissible to pounce on someone for saying something that is incorrect or different. You don't want the hierarchical org chart putting a damper on communicating.

All of this isn't easy to do. It takes work by leadership—leading by example. You have to create an environment that's going to help people feel comfortable to talk, to ask questions and to provide possible solutions, creating an environment of trust where information flows every which way on a daily basis.

▼ PYRAMID PERSPECTIVE:
Trust and Personal Growth

By Jacqui Brady, Client Services
Fellow Ambrosian since July 2008

Trust: It's a powerful concept. By having trust in another individual, you're confident that they have the integrity to follow through on a task, goal or vision. Trust enables you to take a step back and let another individual run the show. As powerful as trust can be when someone has trust in you, even more impact occurs when someone loses trust in you.

A number of years ago Greg Slamowitz and I found ourselves at a roadblock. Management was spearheading the launch of a new initiative, and the mass reaction hadn't gone over as well as we had hoped. In the previous few months, we had let a manager go, and we were experiencing turnover in our department as disengaged employees were leaving for other opportunities. As we replaced these positions with "greener," less experienced candidates, it made sense that these new employees would be afraid to speak up and express their opinions out of fear of retaliation, or so I thought.

I was in my first management position at Ambrose and was looking to prove myself as a competent leader. Looking back, it's clear that I was looking to prove my leadership abilities to the team I was managing rather than to the organization. My priority was the well-being of individuals rather than the well-being of the business, and my actions represented just that.

In one of our team meetings, I offered to take feedback on the latest debatable initiative, and package it, anonymously, to deliver up to management. Since our management team was out of the office at the time attending a conference, I put every-thing into an email and sent it off to Greg. My intentions were to provide him with feedback from the department so Ambrose didn't revert back to the adverse culture we were moving away from under this initiative. However, to Greg, I was disempow-ering my team members by speaking up for them. I refused to attach names to the feedback, as I thought I would then lose trust from my team members. It was a perpetual circle of distrust.

Looking back, while my intentions were in the right place, I went about it the wrong way. I should have taken that meet-ing with my team as an opportunity to encourage everyone to voice their opinions directly to Greg and the rest of manage-ment. I needed to trust that management would appreciate, respect and act on their feedback. The team didn't need me to speak on their behalf; they needed me to encourage them to *feel* comfortable asking questions and providing possible solutions.

At the time, I lacked trust in management. This was before the realization of Ambrose's culture shift, and I didn't believe that the company gave its employees' well-being top priority. At the same time, management was looking to invert the pyramid and my actions actually had acted against that initiative. This negatively impacted Greg's trust in me. He needed to be reassured that I was living Ambrose's core values, supporting inverting the pyramid, and most importantly, leading by example.

Greg and I embraced this circumstance as an opportunity for personal growth. We met biweekly to discuss what happened and how best to move forward. Greg brought to light the details of management's goals for the culture and future wellbeing of Ambrose. After I was provided the opportunity to explain my thought process in my initial actions, it was clear that the two of us were on the same page, working toward the same goal, Ambrose's BHAG. We had simply started from two different ends of the spectrum.

As difficult as it was for us to understand each other in the beginning, we now have an appreciation for the hard work the other has put into Ambrose's cultural and physical growth.

CHAPTER SUMMARY

To be successful and fully empower all of your employees, you need to be obsessed with communicating. It goes hand-in-hand with, and actually activates, the Constitutional Framework, disciplined meeting rhythm, metric literacy and a strong, tribal culture. Communicating is tribal and empowering. People need to know your goals and know the facts in order to participate. People need to learn how to communicate effectively, and be encouraged to do so.

Main chapter points include:

➢ Communicate, communicate, communicate!

➢ Communicate your Constitutional Framework.

➢ Communicate progress.

➤ Communicate change.

➤ Gossip is good as long as it is based upon fact.

➤ Employees need to talk more; leadership needs to listen more.

➤ Besides pumping people full of knowledge, you need to proactively build a culture of trust that has eliminated the fear of retribution.

➤ Command and control structure, under the traditional org chart, inhibits the free flow of information.

➤ When it comes to communicating, management must lead by example.

In the next chapter I discuss building comfort with change, risk and failure; having the right players who embrace personal growth and my most recent area of learning, building an organizational culture of physical and mental wellness and wellbeing.

9 Nourishing Your Culture of Change

Change is good. You need an organizational culture that embraces change. Many people simply aren't comfortable with change, and this has nothing to do with the org chart. This is human nature. People from all levels of the org chart have a hard time with change, emotionally or intellectually, so you need to create an environment that supports, encourages and embraces change. You need to make change easier and more comfortable for people.

For our first 12 years or so in business, there was very little change at Ambrose. All change had to originate from the "top," was micromanaged and was plagued with "analysis paralysis" and fear of failure. Change, whether strategic or tactical, was a difficult, tortuous and emotional process for us. When change did happen, there was an unhealthy obsession, often *post hoc,* over who took credit for it. It was too hard and too draining. Way too much drama. So people (including me) simply gave up and stopped trying to change anything. We disengaged.

We gave up because most people didn't think it was worth the effort. This kind of outlook is not good for any organization. Forward-thinking, creative and solutions-oriented people will mentally and then physically opt out of this type of environment, and without them your business will simply not evolve or improve to better serve your customers and clients.

THE PREREQUISITE: LEADERSHIP'S MIND SHIFT

Here is something leaders struggle with: accepting that change should not be dictated from the top through command and control. Business leaders are not General Patton moving across Europe in 1944. You cannot command and control change. Instead, you need to inspire and encourage it.

The traditional approach to change is all too often a slog. It is slow, laborious and inefficient. It requires brute force. You don't want that. You want change percolating from throughout the company; you want change coming from everywhere and from unexpected places.

As I discussed in Chapter 8, you want everyone's creative right brain working and participating. Leadership doesn't have a lock on creative innovations and solutions. Instead, leadership needs to ask questions and *encourage other folks to come up with creative ideas.* This is a leader's job (also see Vineet Nayar's September 3, 2010 *Harvard Business Review* blog posting on this subject). If leadership had to think of or approve every change, it would never get to its big goals.

Here is great example I got from Tony Hsieh's book *Delivering Happiness.* Let's say we have five people on the senior management team. They each make one change a week for 50 weeks. That amounts to 250 changes or improvements a year. Compare this to the situation where 100 individuals (all of your employees) each make one change or improvement per week—5,000 changes and improvements per year. Which company's going to win? Rather simple. The second company will dust the first company. So, leadership needs to step back and create a positive, supportive environment where folks are empowered and expected to engage in change.

To be honest, I think the preceding example is a bit of an exaggeration. But you get the point. You want changes, big and small, originating from anywhere and anyone. People take incredible pride in effectuating improvements and changes—they will have helped build the organization. How cool is that? Of course, these changes must occur in an aligned manner and be vetted through the disciplined, transparent meeting rhythm.

The point is that people need to know that they are licensed, empowered and expected to effectuate change, and when they do that in a way that is aligned with the organization's Constitutional Framework and goals, leadership must then showcase those people and their innovations as an example for everyone. When you create the structure that I describe in this book, you will be surprised at how much change your organization can handle, especially when it originates from within. I was surprised myself.

But what if there's too much change, you may be asking? First of all, if this is your problem, consider yourself lucky. But worry not. That concern will start to flow through your organization in the disciplined meeting rhythm; it will become apparent and the organization will prioritize and self-adjust. In contrast, if you dictate too much change through command and control, the system will not necessarily self-regulate but become disgruntled and disengaged.

Before an organization can build a culture of change and empower an army of change agents, leaders must understand that they are not the sole provider of ideas and solutions. Good ideas, good solutions and change can—and must—originate from everyone and everywhere. Leadership must be prepared to step aside and watch change happen. They must constantly find, support, celebrate and applaud change led by others, particularly when originating from unexpected, nontraditional places.

Again, you must create that Constitutional Framework, meeting rhythm, metric literacy, an intense tribal culture and an obsession with communicating, and then enable people throughout the company to effectuate changes, both big and small, within that framework.

Do not try to micromanage change. If you try, it will be a miserable slog. Change needs to become part of your tribal mindset.

LEAD BY EXAMPLE

Sometimes I have creative thoughts on how we can innovate our business, and here is what I have found works well for me: I tell folks that I have ideas, but I don't know which ones are good and which ones are bad (also demonstrating our core value of humility), which is why I need other folks at Ambrose to help decide which ones to pursue.

What I am really trying to do here is lead by example. Hey, I am just like everyone else. Let's look at ideas and collectively figure out which ones are good, which ones are bad and how they can be improved, developed and evolved. Also, when we do pursue one of these ideas, I try not to take credit. This is easier to do when you let go of the idea and allow others to morph and improve it, often into something barely recognizable. As a leader and from an ego perspective, yes, it is hard to watch others grow and take ownership of concepts that spring from your creative thoughts, but it works well. Do it, and when others come up with ideas, give their creativity visibility, support and encouragement.

Openly praise solutions, even if small and especially when they come from deep in your organization. This is key. Leaders can do this: creating a big cultural impact and making people feel great.

Too many leaders diminish other people's creativity and solutions, often inadvertently. Do not succumb to the dreaded "smartest person in the room" syndrome and intentionally or unintentionally put down other folks and their ideas. This behavior closes down creativity, change and solutions. People will give up and disengage. We have been there and it is not a good place.

FIND YOUR CHANGE AGENTS

Today, Ambrose is a very different place than it was just four years ago. We are not only comfortable with change; we have culturally, tribally embraced it. We support and encourage change. It has become part of our tribal DNA. The transition did take time and, yes, some folks were apoplectic and some still struggle with change. Fortunately, many people do want to make improvements. It is in their DNA; it is what drives them. However, change is hard. Many forces work against these people, so you need a culture of change to put wind at their backs.

So, how do you create this culture of change? It starts with *change agents*—people within your company who will be instrumental in making change happen.

So how do you find your change agents? By creating an environment that helps these folks emerge and execute. First, as a leader, you need to talk about the importance of change and the acceptance of failure (which I'll discuss later). Build a strong culture of change. Second, you need to visibly praise people who successfully effectuate changes, big and small, especially people who are deep in your organization. Third, you need to educate people about change (send around books and articles on the topic). And fourth, you need to teach people the skills to effectuate change. Lastly, people need to realize that change is engaging and fun. You are giving people the opportunity, and the tools, to build something better.

Believe me, change agents are peppered throughout your organization. As with cultural leaders, find them, love them, support them, embrace them, teach them and liberate them. In the right environment, your change agents will self-select, step forward and lead the team. These are extremely important players on your company's team.

Once your change agents have emerged, you need to teach them how to effectuate change and how to achieve buy-in. This is a critical skill. As I discussed earlier, you cannot just dictate change from the top or through fiat. *Leading Change* and *Buy-In* by John P. Kotter provide very valuable advice for your change agents (more on this later). Another excellent book on the topic is *Switch: How to Change Things When Change Is Hard* by Chip Heath and Dan Heath. There is some great literature on how to manage change.

You also must eliminate the stigma around failure. I like to tell folks that if we don't have failure then we are not trying hard enough. Think of all the failures Edison had before he perfected his light bulb, or how many times even the best baseball sluggers strike out. One of the best books on this topic is *Start-Up Nation* by Dan Senor and Saul Singer. The take-away from this book is Israel's cultural obsession with learning from failure.

I highly encourage you to have all of your change agents—and potential and budding change agents—read these four books. You need to create an army of skilled change agents that is supported by a culture of change and a cultural acceptance of failure.

▼PYRAMID PERSPECTIVE:
Being a Change Agent

By John DeVivo, Sales and Marketing
Fellow Ambrosian since May 2010

I consider myself lucky to have landed at a company like Ambrose for countless reasons. However, one reason sticks out in my mind more than any other: Ambrose is a place where everyone truly believes and embraces the concept that *change is good, and that the people who effect change are also good.*

Change can be an ugly word to some folks in the corporate world, especially in the places I've previously spent time. To some people change is synonymous with various unpleasant feelings, including a lack of comfort, vulnerability, and sometimes just general helplessness. The fear of the unknown, especially when tied to something as important as your career and livelihood, leaves people feeling queasy, and understandably so.

Despite the challenges it presents, it's no secret that change, and the forward movement it precipitates, is paramount to success in today's world. You have to push forward to improve every single aspect of your business, all the time. All of these activities lead to some form of change. Change is a natural by-product of innovation.

Ambrose has worked hard to integrate change into its DNA. We embrace change and the agents who push these changes. We go so far as to teach change through various readings in our library (the book *Switch: How to Change Things When Change Is Hard* by Chip and Dan Heath, and Professor John Kotter's works, come to mind). I've heard that embracing change has not always been easy here at Ambrose. I most likely would not have been able to succeed, or feel as satisfied and engaged as I do currently, at this previous version of Ambrose.

I'm a bit of a "change addict" when it comes to my position. I'm a forward-thinker by nature. I enjoy tinkering with things, trying new stuff, and in general just theorizing about ideas for the future. These are the favorite aspects of my job. Luckily for me, Ambrose embraces this attitude. The company even goes so far as to make sure I'm in situations where I can work toward creating and effecting *more* change. I believe this has been the single most important driver in my overall happiness and success at Ambrose.

By its nature, change "rocks the boat," so it takes uncompromising support from all parts of the organization to make it happen. I have been in countless situations where I've crafted solutions to an issue or proposed a new process that requires a significant amount of change in the way numerous people at the company operate, and I have never been met with anything but rousing support from all the stakeholders involved. This allows us to continue to work toward the "right solutions," and not just the ones that "hurt the least."

Because our culture so truly embraces change, it has unleashed a host of other change agents at the company, so the rate of innovation continues to accelerate. One of my favorite parts about being at a place like this is watching this innovation start as small kernels of ideas, morph over time, and eventually lead to improvements that truly push the company forward. These ideas spring up from every corner of the company.

I have been incredibly fortunate to be in a situation where my natural tendencies and inclination toward thinking ahead mesh perfectly with our company's culture of change. Being embraced as a change agent keeps me super-engaged and excited to tackle whatever lies ahead. Whatever type of change is needed to best move us forward, I know it will be met with enthusiasm and support.

TEACHING CHANGE

This is a concept I gained from the Heath brothers' book *Switch*. Change has two components: emotion and intellect. If you think it's so logical that your company should do something, but you disregard the emotional side, you will most likely fail. Likewise, if you focus only on the emotional side, you will also run into obstacles. You need to teach folks that they have to adequately address both sides: the head and the heart. I wish I had known this earlier in my career.

You have to make sure people can handle and understand change from an emotional and intellectual perspective. Teach your change agents about the elephant and the rider, an Indian proverb. To get the elephant to go in the right direction, the rider (the intellect) and the elephant (the emotion) must work together. They must be aligned. Change often fails because one of these two components was not adequately addressed. Your change agents must understand and master the intellectual and emotional components around change.

Proven tools and processes exist for facilitating change. A formal pro and con analysis is always a helpful and proven business practice. We also use many formal presentations (PowerPoint, video, stakeholder meetings, and so on) that are developed in a team-based, collaborative manner. This approach modulates emotional and intellectual components. We create cross-departmental groups and put a lot of time into presenting to, listening to, and responding to various stakeholders. Stakeholder ideas are visibly sought out and incorporated into initiatives, so that ideas simply become better.

Metrics are helpful, too, in addressing emotional and intellectual components. Folks need to know the facts and that progress, success and failure will be measured and watched. You also need a lot of communication around change, and I really mean a lot. In fact, our large initiatives follow a formal, elaborative, inclusive and communicative "seven-step journey." While the details of this process are beyond the scope of this chapter, a few salient points are worth mentioning here:

➤ Involve all relevant stakeholders throughout the journey.
➤ Vet customer needs and the solution against your Constitutional Framework throughout the journey.

➤ Make sure total transparency exists around the process as well as plenty of metrics and ROI analysis to formally measure success and failure.

➤ Create and execute a formal communication and launch plan.

➤ Also create and execute a formal operations transition and integration plan.

As larger needs and potential solutions originate from throughout the company, put them though this very thorough collaborative and inclusive process, which allows for transparency, stakeholder involvement and buy-in. Communication must occur early and often throughout the process. You need to teach your change agents about building inclusive, tribal teams, incorporating and addressing all stakeholders, tackling the emotional and intellectual components, using metrics and communicating effectively. Your leading change agents must become masters at achieving tribal buy-in to effect change. "Give a man a fish and he will eat for a day; teach a man to fish and he will eat for a lifetime." A truthful proverb, indeed. Your job as a leader is to teach and empower your change agents, and then step back, stand on the sideline and let them play a great game. It is a wonderful game to watch.

CONSTANT FORWARD MOMENTUM

You want a culture of constant change, constant improvement. You want change and improvement to be the norm. You want continuous tribal buy-in, involvement and participation. That requires understanding your people.

Three Types of People

Here is another challenge to change: In any organization, you're going to have three types of people:

➤ Transformers live for change. When properly channeled and encouraged in your organizational structure, they can be golden.

➤ Fence-sitters are cautious and like to observe the change agents, whom they often will end up following, particularly when those

Do You Embrace CHANGE, INNOVATION and EXPERIMENTATION?

◎ What's your comfort level?

◎ The change equation: 5 x 50 = 250 versus 200 x 50 = 10,000

◎ Who are your change agents?

◎ The Elephant and the Rider: Using emotion and intellect

◎ How do you get buy-in?

◎ Transformers, fence-sitters and yes-butters

◎ Don't micromanage change:
Get out of the way.

◎ Celebrate change! It needs to
be tribal!

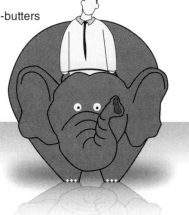

Many moving parts help to nourish change in your organization.

leaders are skilled in involving stakeholders and promoting an in-grained culture of change.

➤ Yes-butters can be potentially debilitating to your organization. They are the ones who always find a reason to fight change. Yes-butters have a role and do need to be listened to and engaged. However, do not let them close down and micromanage all forward momentum. They cannot prevent tactical risk-taking.

The reality is that there is always a reason not to do something, but you need to move past that. The yes-butters will often just get stuck here. They become paralyzed and often trapped in their own logical constructs. When these folks are articulate, and there is not a culture of change or a team of skilled change agents, they have the potential to halt any change and improvement. They become obstructionists, often moving from objection to objection looking for something, anything, to gain traction and to stop forward movement. The Heath brothers, among others, have written about this. I have seen this dynamic at many organizations: our industry trade association, my co-op board, Ambrose. These people are everywhere—Chicken Little proclaiming "the sky is falling."

If you do not have a culture of change and if you do not have skilled change agents, the yes-butters will dominate, instill emotional fear and close down change with their logical constructs. There will be little or no forward momentum. Your clients will suffer the consequences.

Sadly, I have found that many folks with a formal legal education are most often extremely effective yes-butters. (Reminder: I went to law school and practiced the profession for several years.) These folks gravitate toward organizations where leadership doesn't understand the importance of change, where there is no supportive culture of change and few skilled change agents. (This category often includes co-op boards, educational and nonprofit boards and trade associations.) My view is that being an obstructionist is easy, but these folks tend to think they are clever and smart. In contrast, being an effective change agent is a lot harder and way more valuable.

If you are a yes-butter (perhaps even an unaware yes-butter), you can change. I know, because I was a yes-butter for a while, which I believe was largely because of my legal education plus not being in a culture that supported change. However, I have rediscovered the change agent in myself!

The bottom line: Workable and practical solutions that take into account all pros and cons and co-opt stakeholders are the most valuable stock in trade for effective change agents. (I have found a few practicing lawyers with a special skill for weighing all sides and focusing on a way forward, and they are the most valuable advisors.) However, while the yes-butters should be listened to and included in the process like all stakeholders, they cannot be allowed to dominate an organization and stymie all forward change.

Constant Forward Momentum

By Matt Thomas, Legal
Fellow Ambrosian since June 2005

I started at Ambrose in June 2005 as an HR Associate. We were a company made up of roughly 30 people at the time. I was introduced to the Professional Employer Organization (PEO) model at Ambrose and I truly believed in it. Moreover, I believed in Ambrose itself. At the time, when someone asked me what was so great about Ambrose, my response would immediately be "the people!" We took care of each other and our clients.

Here is an example: Two days after starting my job, I received a call from one of our serviced employees who was at the hospital. He had cut his finger with a box-opener and needed his health insurance number while at the emergency room. As the employee's health insurance sponsor, Ambrose had this information. However, my colleagues were all out at client sites and I had absolutely no idea how to get the information this person needed. While on the phone, our COO at the time, Marc Dwek, was walking by, saw my confused look and immediately assisted the employee (and me) throughout the entire process until he was ready for stitches. This was typical of the kind of people and level of service we had at Ambrose.

When I left Ambrose in 2007 to attend law school, the company essentially was the same as it was the day I started. We had great people and we provided excellent service.

Now fast-forward to three years later. I returned to Ambrose to work in our legal department, and I was floored. Talk about forward movement! The company had taken on an incredible change for the better, and our culture had taken a steroid shot. We were still made up of great people who loved to serve, but much more was happening at Ambrose. Ideas were passed around, goals were set and people were excited. It was a creative renaissance!

Greg Slamowitz taught me about transformers, fence-sitters and yes-butters. I noticed that a lot of the yes-butters either departed or had changed their attitudes to become change agents. The great people who loved to serve, but who were yes-butters, kept us in a state of stasis in our early years. It was hard to digest this at first, mainly because I never even knew we were in a state of stasis before I left.

It was only when I returned and I was met with concepts such as metrics, BHAGs, and core values that I realized how much more we had become. These ideas were not something that we had subscribed to (at least as a company) when I was an HR Associate. Now these ideas are ingrained in each of us and naturally push us to constantly think about how we can serve our clients better.

One of my favorite quotations from Greg is "we are never done." I think we all subscribe to that point of view. It is the potential of *what can be* that makes Ambrose special—and that is simply awesome.

FAILURE IS OKAY

When you create a culture where change is accepted, where it is encouraged, embraced and expected, you also need to have a tolerance for risk-taking and failure.

Yes-butters will obsess over failure. They will get very dramatic and use it to prove their point that no change can happen. They will say, "See, see, I told you so! I was right and you were wrong." (Hmm, perhaps it is all about them and their ego?) Yes-butters fear change, and if they rule the roost change will simply not happen, or it will be extremely slow and tortuous.

To deal with yes-butters you need to create a cultural narrative: *Change is good, and although some things will fail, that is okay. We can learn from failure, and besides, if we don't have failure, we aren't trying hard enough.*

Yes-butters are generally perplexed by this narrative. As a leader, you need to give your change agents cultural cover and support. That's because when they eventually fail at something the yes-butters will be all over them, calling for their heads.

Yes-butters want to send folks who fail to Siberia. Yes-butters want the change agents to sit in the proverbial corner with a dunce cap. You cannot allow this to happen. You need to flip failure on its face. In the context of striving for positive change, failure is good, providing it is above the water line. *Great try. What did you learn? Let's try again!*

What Did You Learn?

The book *Start-Up Nation* by Dan Senor and Saul Singer, mentioned previously, is an excellent read about the Israeli military and entrepreneurial economy. The authors believe that the reason the Israeli economy is so entrepreneurial is because of their cultural view, which comes from the Israeli military's cultural obsession over studying and learning from each and every failure. Senor and Singer tell us that failure for the Israelis is all about what they learned. This is the type of narrative you must ingrain in your company's psyche to prevent yes-butters from boxing down your change agents and blocking any forward momentum.

In the United States, unlike Israel, we have a deep stigma around failure. We are obsessed with assigning blame. In contrast, according to Senor and Singer, whenever the Israeli army has a disastrous encounter, a commission convenes, often before the battle is over, to study what went wrong in order to learn and improve. This Israeli army mentality has carried over into their business culture.

We don't have enough of that in the United States. Despite our stigma of failure, great organizations build an acceptance around failure into their corporate culture. It's not easy and it takes substantial self-awareness and strong leadership. So whenever somebody makes a mistake, I always like to ask them, with a smile on my face, *what did you learn?*

ARE YOU A CHANGE AGENT?

I've already asked if you are a cultural leader, and now I ask, *are you a change agent?* Your company needs cultural leaders, and lots of change agents too. Both are vital people in any organization. If you do yet not know who they are, pay close attention and create an environment that will help them to emerge and shine. They are there; they just might need some support. Celebrate them.

CHAPTER SUMMARY

You need an organizational culture that embraces change. However, many folks simply are not comfortable with it, so you need to make change easier for them.

Main chapter points include:

➤ You need to create an environment that supports, encourages and embraces change.

➤ Create a comfort level with change.

➤ Leadership needs to ask many questions and encourage other folks to come up with creative ideas.

➤ Do not try to micromanage change. Change needs to become part of your tribal mindset.

➤ Openly praise solutions, even if small, and especially when they come from deep in your organization.

➤ Change agents exist throughout your organization. You need to find them, love them, embrace them, teach them and liberate them.

➤ Eliminate the stigma around failure. If you don't have any failure, then you are not trying hard enough.

➤ Successful change requires both an emotional and an intellectual perspective.

➤ Be aware of transformers, fence-sitters and yes-butters. They will impact your success in effecting change.

➤ Build a culture of change. Celebrate it.

We've now explored the Constitutional Framework, a disciplined meeting rhythm, metric literacy, a strong, tribal culture, an organizational obsession with communication, and a culture embracing and supporting of risk, failure and change. In the next chapter, I discuss how these concepts apply to your sales and marketing efforts.

10

A Word About Sales and Marketing

The focused application of the key methodologies I've discussed in this book will profoundly transform your sales and marketing group. That certainly was our experience.

To assure that your company has a similar outcome you must turn your back on command and control. That's not easy for most entrepreneurs. In fact, it wasn't easy for us. We had our yes-butters, and you will as well, but don't let them slow you down. Change your organizational ways, intensely focusing on (repeat after me) your Constitutional Framework, clearly defined and objectively measurable goals, a disciplined meeting rhythm, metrics literacy, an obsession with communication, a strong tribal culture that embraces and supports change, and of course awesome human capital. Within this construct, you will liberate your sales and marketing people to focus on your goals. You will move toward places that were simply unfathomable through command and control. It may take some time, but have confidence and patience in this approach. It is a proven methodology.

When we founded Ambrose we knew absolutely nothing about sales or marketing (although we thought we knew everything). Simply, we thought all you needed to do was get in front of folks and talk a lot about our great service offering. We didn't ask a prospect about his or her needs. We didn't want to know and we didn't really care. Trying to sell ice to Eskimos was fine. A lot of brute force and individual Herculean effort was all that was necessary. So we thought.

For Ambrose's first 12 years, we thought we knew how to sell and how to build a sales organization—hire sales folks and have them do what we did, just get out there, meet as many people as possible and tell them how great we are, with conviction. We thought we knew everything there was to know about sales, but we did not have an inkling of how to build a first-class sales and marketing operation. The "smartest person in the room" syndrome held us back yet again. We didn't know what we didn't know. To compound the situation, we managed through command and control, barking ridiculous orders at people. It was a painful, ugly slog that depended on brute force and heroic individual efforts. It was hard, unpleasant and unscalable.

NEW BEGINNINGS

Those early years radically contrast with what transpired once we admitted we knew nothing and organizationally pivoted. We built our Constitutional Framework and put into practice the other necessary organizational components discussed in this book. We abandoned command and control and allowed and encouraged great human capital to stretch, learn, grow, experiment and generally excel in their contributions to our organization's sales and marketing efforts.

This is not rocket science. These are very practical and proven approaches, if done correctly. Great sales and marketing people operating within this book's organizational constructs will execute these approaches beautifully.

Once we liberated our superb sales and marketing human capital, allowing our people to self-actualize, we encouraged them to attend seminars and training sessions, as well as read plenty of books and articles. Here are a few of the books that got us tactically going in the right direction:

➤ *SPIN Selling* by Neil Rackham

➤ *The Ultimate Sales Machine* by Chet Holmes

➤ *The Inside Advantage* and *The New Experts*, both by Robert H. Bloom

➤ *Inbound Marketing* by Brian Halligan, Dharmesh Shah and David Meerman Scott

➤ *Real-Time Marketing and PR* by David Meerman Scott

➤ *All Marketers ~~Are Liars~~ Tell Stories* by Seth Godin

➤ *Reality Marketing Revolution* by Eric Keiles and Mike Lieberman

➤ *Different: Escaping the Competitive Herd* and other titles by Youngme Moon

There are many more. Find them and apply the principles discussed in this book. There's no need to reinvent the wheel in this area.

NOT THE SMARTEST PERSON IN THE ROOM

A few year back, Hugh LaRoche, one of our top sales associates who was promoted to head of our sales and marketing group (although at that time we actually had absolutely no marketing group), joined me in attending a two-day sales and marketing conference put on by Verne Harnish. (Unfortunately, Verne no longer hosts this particular conference, which was solely dedicated to sales and marketing.) Verne had put together two great days of presentations by leading sales and marketing gurus (Chet Holmes, David Meerman Scott and Bob Bloom, Greg Alexander, to name a few). We were deer in headlights. While I suspected that we didn't know much about sales and marketing, thus the reason for this sojourn, after the morning session, Hugh and I looked at each and simultaneously said, "We know nothing!" It was a refreshing realization. You need to know what you don't know.

The Five Tiers of Sales

Greg Alexander, CEO of Sales Benchmark Index, whose firm we now use (a testament to the power of education-based selling), gave an excellent presentation that same morning, outlining the five stages of a sales organization. Greg explained to us that the top tier is a well-oiled, integrated, multidimensional and dynamic sales and marketing machine. As Chet Holmes put it, your sales folks are fully supported by an "ultimate sales machine."

SALES MANAGEMENT MATURITY MODEL (SM3)

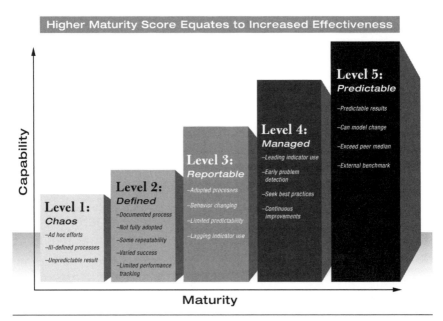

We're striving to work our way up the five stages of a sales organization. (Credit: Sales Benchmark Index)

Greg Alexander described the concept of shift and lift. *Shift* lead generation away from your sales folk, then *lift* them up and present them to the prospect. It boils down to building an incredibly efficient sales and marketing engine that supports your sales people, removes and automates mundane and routine processes, and allows them to spend as much time as possible effectively engaging prospective customers. You want to constantly study each activity performed by your sales people in detail. You must figure out which activities can be removed from the individual sales person and placed in a more cost-effective and more efficient location. There you can then have someone intensely focus on it, measure it and constantly improve it. This approach enables you to build an eight-piston BMW cruising down the autobahn at 110 miles per hour.

On the bottom tier of Greg Alexander's sales and marketing pyramid is the early-stage entrepreneur reliant on pure grit, adrenaline and heroics—cold calling, developing and doing the closing—all alone, or worse, hiring talented sales folks and dictating to them to do the same. No business process support and no marketing support. This is a one-piston jalopy (at best) on the autobahn jittering along as fast as possible. Not a pleasant drive.

Twelve years into Ambrose, we were still in the bottom tier, although Hugh and I did agree we were in the top part of the bottom tier (after 12 years, big whoop). We had great sales people and excellent client service, which was a critically important source of referrals for years. (This is a *sine qua non* for everything discussed in this chapter.) But that was it, and it was not enough to build a scalable first-class sales and marketing organization.

We realized that we needed to flip the pyramid and unleash our human capital. The sales and marketing part of our business was micromanaged from the top, total command and control, and our great human capital in that group was not allowed to self-actualize—to change, stretch, experiment and evolve.

At this point, we had to do two things to radically transform the sales and marketing group. First, we had to continue to build our Constitutional Framework, add the disciplined meeting rhythm, increase our dependence on metrics, build a stronger tribal culture, and allow for experimentation, risk, change and failure. Second, we then needed to liberate our human capital within this organizational construct, inject good proven ideas into the group and let them figure how to meet our objective goals.

As I have mentioned in previous chapters, this wasn't simply about letting go. To stop micromanaging without anything to fill the void wasn't and isn't the answer. As I've noted, you also need to build that Constitutional Framework and put into place the proven business practices that I have described in this book. Only then will you liberate your human capital in an aligned manner.

It took us three years to effectuate this organizational transformation and to methodically move from the bottom of the Greg Alexander's sales and marketing pyramid to the top. While I don't think we have made it yet to the very top, we are getting close.

This was a huge transformation for us—a tribal journey—and everyone had fun along the way. It certainly was a very different experience than the previous command and control slog.

APPLYING THE CONSTITUTIONAL FRAMEWORK

Embracing a Constitutional Framework, core values, metrics, brand promise, change, failure and regular meeting rhythm—using these principals as your guide—you'll find that you can have an amazing positive impact on sales and marketing. In fact, you can have an amazing positive impact on every area of your organization. For us, taking our core value of "to Teach and to be Taught" to task, we looked outside of Ambrose and learned as much as we could about sales and marketing. In addition to hiring Greg Alexander's company, we also hired Brian Halligan and Dharmesh Shah's firm HubSpot (www.hubspot.com), another testament to the power of education-based selling.

The following are just a few of the tactical, very iterative activities that our liberated human capital has undertaken in the last three years within our *Flip the Pyramid* organizational construct:

> **Education-Based Selling and Thought Leadership:** A significant education-based selling program (educational seminars, presentations, panels, webinars, whitepapers, conferences, blogging, writing this book, and more).

> **Focused and Dynamic Branding:** A dynamic and rich web presence; ongoing branding efforts within our client verticals.

> **Inbound Marketing:** A robust inbound marketing program that includes search engine optimization, search engine marketing campaigns, blogging and various forms of social media.

> **Outbound Marketing:** Tailored and targeted electronic email and outbound campaigns.

➢ **Activity and Results Tracking:** A sophisticated sales and marketing activity and classification tracking management system with a heavy focus on metrics.

➢ **Hiring and Coaching the Best People:** A heightened focus on hiring the best sales people (the addition of "Topgrading"); continual coaching in needs-based selling techniques; a focus on physical and mental wellbeing.

▼ PYRAMID PERSPECTIVE:
Building a Sales Machine

By Hugh LaRoche, Sales and Marketing
Fellow Ambrosian since March 2005

How are we ever going to make this work?

At the end of 2008 and early 2009 the economic sky was falling. The financial markets were in upheaval and the U.S. economy was on the precipice of another Great Depression. Companies everywhere were struggling to survive as sales were down and credit markets severely tightened up. Fear and uncertainty reigned as unemployment began to skyrocket. Ambrose, however, was doing an admirable job of maintaining slow but steady growth. In recognition of the times and our position relative to other companies we often joked, "Flat is the new growth!"

As the newly minted head of sales, I dreamed of helping Ambrose reach new heights, but feared that the pervading macroeconomic conditions could thwart even the best of efforts. Fortunately, my promotion coincided with a cultural shift within our organization. This shift was based on recognizing our need for organizational alignment, and was codified by our core values: Humility, Respect, Dedication, Integrity, Excellence, and to Teach and be Taught—our HR diet. The last of these values would prove particularly vital, for though I had always flourished in sales, translating that success across an organization would call on a very different skill set. It was time to go get "taught" and not make the fatal mistake of believing myself to be the smartest person in the room.

The good news was that we were starting off with a strong foundation. We had always known that, if nothing else, we had to focus on bringing in great people. But how would we most effectively leverage our talent?

We took one *giant* leap forward when Greg Slamowitz and I attended a Verne Harnish Sales and Marketing conference in New Orleans in early 2009, and I do mean *giant!* We learned about an entirely different and much more sophisticated approach to sales. Startled by how much we didn't know, we began drinking from the proverbial fire hose.

Not only was the conference an eye-opener, but we also discovered many books that tied directly into what we were trying to accomplish. Greg, knowing that I was a notoriously reluctant reader, pushed me to read more business books in the next six months than I had read in the entirety of my academic career. I am ever thankful for his "encouragement," as to this day I rely on them as my foundation for leadership and as a roadmap for achieving our goals.

One book in particular that captured the essence of what we were trying to accomplish on the sales growth front was Chet Holmes' *The Ultimate Sales Machine.* That book taught me that you need great people and a great system of "shift and lift" to help those people maximize their results. Don't drown a highly compensated sales executive in administrative tasks and hope that he or she will remember to do all the marketing, analysis and follow up. Free that person up so that he or she can do what they do best—close deals! The lessons in *The Ultimate Sales Machine* reinforced everything that I had learned from my academic experience, and I was excited at the opportunity to be the architect of Ambrose's new sales effort.

For more than a decade, we had been working with a series of "one-piston engines," namely the sales executives. Finally, we began to build a multi-piston sales engine that included analyst support, marketing and a robust customer relationship management (CRM) system from SalesForce that was customized to our needs. Sales picked up and optimism began to grow.

I wish I could simply say at this point "and we lived happily ever after," but that was not the case. Building the sales machine was (and still is) an iterative process with some bumps and bruises along the way. Additionally, change can often be difficult for any organization, and ours was no different. There will always be those who would rather stand back and tell you why something won't work rather than suggest alternatives or even try new options.

Fortunately, along with our cultural revolution (as I often like to call it), Ambrose was also in the midst of a metrics revolution as well. Having done my MBA studies at a very quantitatively driven program, I had always taken comfort in numbers, and relied on them to help inform direction. Sales naturally lends itself to metrics, and they really helped ensure that we stayed on the right track. Are our chosen options really working? Are they worth the necessary investment? Are we on pace to meet our targets? With metrics, we were able to answer these questions quickly and march toward our goals with aplomb.

Even after methodically building out a sales and marketing team from scratch, geographically diversifying our new business and achieving record sales numbers year after year, all in what would be described as, at best, a "soft economy," there are still those that will attribute our success to "good timing" or just plain "good luck." But isn't that the nature of success in general?

How much should one ascribe to hard work versus pure serendipity? I don't know the answer, but I do know this: While it's important to have a plan for hitting goals and critical to do post-

> analysis, it is not wise to focus solely on results. In other words, it's not just about the destination. The journey is the key! We continue to be vigilant in staying true to our core values, core purpose, brand promise and our Big Hairy Audacious Goal. I believe as long as we do so, we will do more than simply hit our stated objectives; we will achieve more than we ever dreamed.

EXPERIMENTATION, METRICS AND GOALS

We measure every aspect of our sales and marketing efforts and are constantly experimenting with new techniques and approaches, keeping and tweaking what works and changing or jettisoning what doesn't. No need to get emotional. This is a constant process and is an important component of a vibrant sales and marketing organization. You do not want to command and control this, but you do want it to be part of the DNA of your sales and marketing group. You want this to happen every single day and it cannot be micromanaged from the "top."

Goals, experimentation and metrics are the difference between selling by brute force and selling with skilled confidence. The latter is a well-oiled dynamic and constantly evolving sales and marketing machine supporting smart, well-trained sales folks. I am reminded of the Albert Einstein quote, "Insanity is doing the same thing over and over again and expecting a different result." We finally stopped doing the same thing over and over again. What a difference.

Our 15th year in business, the first full sales year after our sales and marketing transformation, was our best sales year ever by a very significant margin (with new sales up 60 percent). I can attest that the top of Greg Alexander's sales and marketing pyramid is a lot better than the bottom. It did take us three years of dedication, experimentation and focus to move up the sales and marketing pyramid, but once you get toward the top, you want to stay there. You can feel the difference; it is actually a lot easier.

CHAPTER SUMMARY

Sales and marketing are among the most critical functions of any business, and can be improved particularly through the focused application of your Constitutional Framework, disciplined meeting rhythm, metric literacy, strong tribal culture, an organizational obsession with communication, a culture that embraces and supports change, and of course your BHAG.

Main chapter points include:

➤ To reach the top tier in sales and marketing, you need a well-oiled, integrated, multidimensional and dynamic sales and marketing machine that is constantly evolving.

➤ Success in sales and marketing requires acknowledging that you aren't the smartest folks in the room and finding out what you *do not know* about sales and marketing.

➤ Experimentation and metrics are important components of a vibrant sales and marketing organization.

➤ You need to liberate awesome sales and marketing human capital within a strong Constitutional Framework and religiously put into practice the other organizational components discussed in this book.

In the next chapter, I discuss the importance of building an organizational culture of physical and mental wellness and wellbeing.

11

Great People and the Importance of Wellness

You create your Constitutional Framework—complete with core values, BHAG, core purpose, brand promise and annual and quarterly goals. You then bring it to life with a disciplined meeting rhythm, metric literacy, a strong tribal culture, an obsession with communicating and an acceptance of change and risk. Of course, it all requires the key ingredient of great people.

You must recruit, retain and develop great people in this organizational construct. For example, you need to ask yourself, "Do I have people who embrace personal growth?" While generally A players attract A players, and B players attract C players, in my experience it is more complex than this.

Here's the thing: The right culture, the right environment and the right Constitutional Framework can turn B+ players into A players. With the right atmosphere, you can get the best out of each person, including your A players. As a leader, and as an organization, you must place an incredible amount of time, energy and resources into attracting, retaining and developing great people—those who want to engage and excel in this type of positive organizational construct. You must recruit people who *want* to be engaged, empowered, aligned and on fire.

In my opinion, this is not optional if you want to build a winning team. Anyone not interested must get off the bus now (preferably they won't get on in the first place). Recruiting great players *who want to engage* must become a top priority for the organization. "Where People Count" is one of our mottos at Ambrose, and "Great People" is one of the three prongs of our brand promise. A top company goal is to recruit great people who want to engage, and to then deliver to these folks a great, engaging experience. This isn't easy to do, and it is something I constantly worry about.

SO WHO IS AN A PLAYER?

Let me back up for a moment and give you our rather broad definition of the type of person we consider to be an A player: An A player embraces our core values and our culture. This is foremost and non-negotiable. It is also very important for an A player to have an excellent skill set for his or her position. Finally, an A player is aligned, engaged, empowered and achieving at his or her peak performance level.

To create a winning team of A players, you must have a confluence of the following:

➣ Great human capital that wants to engage.

➣ The right people in the right positions.

➣ A strong Constitutional Framework.

➣ A strong, supportive culture that sets everyone up for success.

According to this definition, a great Constitutional Framework and a great culture can turn a B+ player into an A player. So, you need both a great environment and willing players to create a winning team. One without the other is just not enough.

TURNING A "B+" INTO AN "A"

I want to share a short story from when I was a youth. I am, and always have been, a mediocre athlete, the proverbial B+ player. I played various team sports and generally had terrible to fair experiences, with one exception. One year, while in junior high school, I played on a soccer team in my hometown league and had an exceptional coach, Bruce Dunnan. He had recently graduated from Rutgers, where he played soccer.

Coach Dunnan was disciplined and trained us hard. He focused on developing the skills of every player, not just those of the talented players. Consequently, every player improved during the season. Coach Dunnan was also positive and encouraging. His approach was to get the best out of each of us emotionally and intellectually. He put a great emphasis on team-building and creating positive team dynamics. Under Coach Dunnan, we enjoyed a lot of camaraderie and celebration.

After many average coaches, I felt that I finally had a great coach. What a difference, especially for the B+ player that I was. I gained confidence, pushed myself to my limit and was totally committed to the team. I was playing by far the best soccer of my life and I felt great about it. I loved our team and gave it my all.

That season we went to the championship game (in retrospect, no surprise). The score was tied one to one and in the second half I found myself all alone downfield. A teammate passed the ball to me (and it is significant that a teammate felt confident passing to a mediocre player in the championship game with a tied score). I stopped the ball, focused and set myself up for a textbook kick toward the goal. A confident, solid kick.

I scored the winning goal. My teammates mobbed me in celebration. I felt awesome. Coach Dunnan set each of his players up for success. He knew how to get the best out of each of us, not just his stars. Coach Dunnan turned B+ players into A players. Coach Dunnan turned me into an A player. This is the type of experience that leadership must deliver to every person at their company. But you do need people who want this type of engaging experience. This is how you win the championship game with style.

Finding the Match

As I have discussed, everybody employed with your company must have a cultural and core value match. This is not negotiable. Your culture and core values must be so apparent on your website and in your company's blog that you have people affirmatively opting into joining your company and its mindset. People often read my blog or attend one of my presentations and then reach out to us for employment opportunities.

These people are asking to join our tribe. They want an engaging experience. This is important, but you also need a skill set match. You want a lot of mentoring, coaching, teaching and learning. You want to create a real learning environment where people are encouraged, *and expected,* to stretch, learn and grow. For example, I am constantly emailing around links to articles and books on a weekly basis. We also encourage people to change roles and positions. All job opening are first posted internally. We want people to read, think, and try new approaches and to fully engage their colleagues and our tribe. This is a top priority for Ambrose.

THE SELECTION PROCESS

Our interviewing process is rigorous. It usually requires that candidates meet at least ten people in the first round. Then, if they get past that round of interviews, we have them come back for an intense "Topgrading" interview, an in-depth forensic process developed by Jeff and Brad Smart and conducted by experts professionally trained in the technique. Topgrading interviews generally last at least four hours, with a methodology that helps you more easily and accurately identify top performers. Ambrose is very disciplined and highly selective in its interviewing process. (Just ask anyone who has been through it.) You are interviewed for cultural alignment, desire to engage and skill set.

Tension often exists between meeting our hiring goals and remaining disciplined in our approach. On a few occasions, even recently, we have compromised our rigorous selection process to meet a hiring goal and have almost invariably ended up making a hiring mistake. These hiring mistakes, at minimum, cost time and money.

In fact, recently we compromised our hiring processes, specifically around cultural alignment and willingness to engage, as we tried to find somebody for a hard-to-fill tech position. It resulted in a glaring mismatch. What was surprising to me was that this fellow knew how important culture and core values were to us, and he simply didn't show up for my cultural orientation class for new hires. No advance notice. His excuse was that he was busy.

After five months, he abruptly quit with no notice and stated in his letter that the reason was irreconcilable differences with Ambrose's culture. We obviously should not have hired this individual. He had spent most of his career as an independent contractor and had little experience as a team player, and once we figured out the cultural mismatch we should have separated from him. This was a mistake, and again we were reminded of the importance of following our disciplined hiring process.

AVOID CULTURAL MEDIOCRITY

Unfortunately, based on my personal experience, I have noticed that trade associations, co-op boards and nonprofits too often have weak or nonexistent Constitutional Frameworks. They also tend to lack vibrant, positive cultures and often have little or no discipline around the selection of their human capital, particularly volunteers. The absence of these components causes frustration, inefficiency and a lot of petty nonsense—a recipe for dysfunction and failure.

These organizations also often take all, or most, volunteers. Participation, voluntary and hired, is sometimes controlled by the B and C players who are more focused on their personal egos and personal agendas than on the overall success of the organization. These B and C players generally lack the mindset, the understanding and the skill set to turn the B+ players into A players. Meanwhile, A players will opt out of such dysfunctional organizations, leaving the B players to dominate and not advance in their skills or aspire to A-player status. Worse, the B players will then recruit C players, creating a repository of mediocre and weak B and C players.

I believe that this is a significant reason why many trade associations and voluntary organizations are sometimes dysfunctional, frustrating and inefficient—it certainly has been my experience.

So, this is the downside of working with top performers in an aligned, engaged and empowered organization—you know how great it is! I suggest that when you partner with nonprofit and volunteer organizations you pay special attention to core values, culture and their recruitment processes. There *are* some excellent nonprofits that do "get it," and you should seek these out.

Of course, you do not want your own organization to become a repository of weak B and C players. It's a disaster, so avoid the trap. You want A players who, along with strong leadership, turn B+ players into more A players.

The old game of B players making themselves "look good" by surrounding themselves with C players is a losing strategy, and you do not want to play that game. To the contrary, you want aligned, engaged and empowered A players and B+ players who strive to become A players, all of whom are reaching their full potential while having a great personal and tribal experience.

That is how you win the championship.

THE IMPORTANCE OF WELLNESS

You work on creating and tweaking the right organizational construct that gets the best out of everyone. You then recruit and retain great human capital with a desire to engage and grow, encouraging your team players to excel. What's next? Achieving excellent mental and physical health by creating an organizational "culture of wellness" while providing the tools and incentives to encourage it.

This is the most recent part of Ambrose's organizational journey, and one that currently has created a lot of tribal excitement. Think about it. This isn't simply about people and their experience at work. *This is about people and their experience in life.* We have begun creating a culture of wellness by providing tools and support structures to help people achieve better mental and physical wellbeing.

A fair number of large companies have ventured down this road with a lot of success (L.L. Bean, Johnson & Johnson, American Express, Dow Chemical, Green Mountain Coffee, Pitney Bowes, Eastman Chemical, Caterpillar and Lincoln Industries, among others). These companies have strategically and tactically built a culture of wellness. This is a huge deliverable to your employees and their families.

▼PYRAMID PERSPECTIVE:

Finding a Healthy Work-Life Balance

By Ariel Merkrebs-Finkelstein, Client Services
Fellow Ambrosian since August 2011

Similar to training for a marathon, the recipe for professional success typically comprises two core ingredients: training and dedication (and perhaps a dash of knowledge). When I first began my job, like many new employees I found myself exercising my brain more than my muscles. I incorrectly assumed that if I got in early, stayed late and over-exerted myself *mentally*, I would perform at my best and perhaps even receive an Employee of the Month nomination.

Unfortunately, while this approach accelerated my proficiency, it came at the cost of inadvertently putting my important day-to-day activities, such as exercising, on hold. Essentially, I focused on *doing* well as opposed to *being* well, instead of balancing these two imperatives.

When working for a company like Ambrose, which prides itself on teamwork and a healthy work-life-balance, such tunnel vision does not last long. With an annual Health and Wellness Fair, internal fitness competitions facilitated by complimentary pedometers and fruit-salad birthday feasts, it is nearly impossible to neglect caring for yourself amidst the company's strong health-conscious community. At Ambrose, the concept of wellness includes more than just the physical; it encompasses all aspects of maintaining a healthy work-life balance including (but not limited to) knowledge, exercise, nutrition and access to health insurance.

Surrounding myself with healthy, hard-working professionals transformed my metaphorical recipe and showed me that it is possible to achieve professional successes while simultaneously supporting and protecting physical and mental health.

For example, I ran in this past year's Wall Street 5K, and even won a prize through our internal walking challenge. I also regularly use my health insurance for preventative visits, such as annual checkups and semi-annual teeth cleanings, and I reap financial rewards from my healthcare provider through gift cards for these visits.

Inevitably my 180-degree transformation can be attributed to several factors, but none more noteworthy than Ambrose's culture, and the people who strengthen it. Collectively, they foster individual wellness and create a support system that enables a superior work-life balance. As a result, I find myself refreshed and eager to come into the office, performing at a level I had not anticipated just one short year ago.

I now realize that working in a fast-paced environment in many ways parallels the rigors of training for a marathon. In one sense, the challenges of achieving a comfortable personal-professional tradeoff transcend this simple metaphor, but nonetheless, like a marathon, workplace balance requires practice and training while you also attend to your own personal needs, lest you burn out from sprinting too fast. Ambrose has taught me the importance of wellness via a healthy work-life balance and, for that, I feel empowered by my job and I am appreciative for the lessons I learn while an Ambrose employee.

DISCOVERING A WELLNESS POLICY

During the summer of 2009, while the United States House of Representatives was crafting its healthcare legislation (known as The Affordable Care Act or Obamacare), I printed out and read the entire bill—all 3,000-plus pages. It was a slog. Later that fall, I had also printed out and read the comparable healthcare bill that had been moving through the United States Senate. While there were significant differences between the House and the Senate versions, and the Senate bill ultimately became law, both versions contained potentially transformational wellness provisions that were not being discussed in the press.

These provisions and the public policy behind them intrigued me, so I started to learn as much as I could about corporate wellness programs. On my own dime, I continued to read, study, learn and attend conferences on this topic.

As a result, I have become well-versed on this topic, invested personally in an early-stage company in this space and am excited to report that Ambrose has just recently begun building a culture of wellness that, so far, is being enthusiastically embraced by the Ambrose tribe.

WHY WELLNESS?

The United States currently spends 17.9 percent of its gross domestic product on healthcare. Our peer group of other developed countries spends nine percent, with better outcomes. Our current national healthcare spending is unsustainable, is a drag on real wages and increases the cost of goods and services, which makes us globally uncompetitive. What is also alarming is that we have serious mental and physical health issues associated with lifestyle, and these issues are getting worse (for example, the growing Type II diabetes pandemic).

So, we are creating significant healthcare costs by choice. These lifestyle-related health issues are in fact a significant drain on our economy and our nation's wellbeing. Exorbitant employee healthcare spending is taking financial resources from cash compensation, capital improvements and shareholder return. This is not good for the United States.

Ask yourself "Has my company faced eight, ten or twelve percent or more annual healthcare cost increases over the last decade?" Shouldn't U.S. companies use this money for employee pay increases, to invest in new products or services, new equipment, to reduce their debt, or to increase retained earnings or shareholder distributions? The leading thinking is that well-designed and administered wellness programs and a strong culture of wellness can bend our nation's healthcare cost curve and create more productive employees living richer lives.

Wellness has the potential to also significantly drive down our national healthcare spending and deliver better, healthier outcomes. I highly recommend reading Professor Clayton Christensen's book, *The*

Innovator's Prescription, which analyzes strategies to improve healthcare and make it affordable.

Besides draining cash from our national economy and America's employers and employees, poor mental and physical health will affect your company's performance. I look at it this way: As the coach, general manager or team owner, you want your players in their best mental and physical shape. In fact, as a nation, don't we want our nation's human capital in the best mental and physical shape to best compete in the global arena?

If your people are trying to work despite health issues (the HR term for this is *presenteeism*), they lose their ability to focus, engage and perform to their best abilities. Look at it this way: Your employees are athletes. They need to be in great mental and physical health to play a great, engaging game at work and thrive overall in their lives.

In the United States, healthcare is principally delivered to people through employers. The cost of this alone is a good reason for you to actively support physical and mental health. However, another more important reason is that as a leader you should want everyone to achieve his or her full human potential. People cannot achieve their potential if they have poor or even fair mental and physical health. So, you need to tactically and strategically encourage them to improve this aspect of their lives. This approach toward human capital, your most important asset, is just another way to genuinely engage employees—to create an environment where they can excel. It will empower your company, and our nation, to break away from competitors.

WELLNESS ROI

Leading studies demonstrate the significant return on investment for well-designed and administered wellness programs, and for building a culture of wellness. Katherine Baicker, professor of health economics at Harvard, and her colleagues calculate that each $1 spent on well-designed and administered wellness programs produces a return on investment of $3.27 for medical cost savings and $2.73 for absenteeism reduction.

This is astounding. Well-designed, promoted and administered employer-based health plans and wellness programs reduce health and disability insurance costs, increase employee engagement and productivity and have a positive effect on an organization's culture. In my opinion, this journey is not optional for each of us and for our nation as a whole.

AMBROSE'S EXPERIENCE

Ambrose is embracing wellness with a vengeance. For years, wellness for us was providing a $600 per year gym membership stipend. We had absolutely no metrics on the impact of this spending. We had no idea who went to the gym, who didn't, and whether or not it had a measurable impact on our mental and physical health. There was little or no excitement or tribal motivational effect from this wellness investment. We recently modified this benefit by purchasing for everyone a device called a Fitbit, which, among other things, measures your daily steps and physical activity and posts it on a personalized Internet dashboard.

Through the Fitbit website, we have created a group challenge called Rock Da 'Brose, complete with a group leader board. Metrics and transparency. We added monetary rewards, including a gym stipend for folks who reach certain activity goals, as well as public celebration of leaders and winners. What is amazing is that our wellness spending has dropped by a third. So far, this program has had a huge positive impact on our overall physical activity and tribal bonding.

The Ambrose Fitbit challenge has become a company-wide obsession with a lot of competition, chatter, celebration, focus on the leader board and, most importantly, a lot of physical activity across the company. People are now pacing at their desks, going out for power walks at lunch, holding walking meetings, and are getting off one or two subway stops early. While this is just one type of company-wide wellness initiative, we intend to experiment with many others as time goes on.

We are exploring some additional wellness initiatives. For example:

➤ Healthy cooking and eating classes.

➤ Exercise/shower facility.

> ➤ Increasing the "rebate" paid for participating in the annual Health Risk Assessment.

> ➤ Providing health insurance premium "rebates" for meeting specific targeted health outcomes, such as cholesterol, body mass index (BMI), blood sugar/glucose levels and blood pressure.

> ➤ Providing health insurance premium "rebates" for participation in relevant wellness programs for people with high cholesterol, unhealthy BMI, high sugar/glucose levels, and high blood pressure.

> ➤ Providing an economic incentive for tobacco users to participate in tobacco cessation programs.

If you do this properly, and with the proper communication and organizational buy-in, you can build a culture of wellness where folks become excited about improving their personal mental and physical wellbeing. I am also confident that Ambrose will figure out how to deliver effective wellness programs to its small business clients as well. This is the newest and most recent leg in our journey.

▼PYRAMID PERSPECTIVE:
Investing In Wellness

By Kyle Grubman, Product Development
Fellow Ambrosian since November 2011

Before the sun rises I am on a bus to beat the morning rush. Roughly 75 minutes later I arrive at the office. After a solid day of work, I am back on a bus to return home. Often using the commute as an excuse, I overeat at dinner and go straight to bed, only to wake up the next morning to do it all over again.

For my first few months working at Ambrose, I repeated that cycle, much like most of America. A poor diet and little activity resulted in depleted energy levels and significant weight gain. I remember running on the treadmill at the gym. I turned to a side mirror and saw a stranger. I did not recognize myself.

The Heath brothers write in their book *Switch* that "self-control is an exhaustible resource." I did not become an overweight, fatigued "stranger" intentionally. I wanted to do better, but had little energy to make the tough choices. For many, work is probably high on the list of self-control challengers.

I refuse to accept that premise any longer. What if we turned that scenario on its head? What if people went to work to not only conserve their self-control, but even recharge it?

That's how I see wellness and why my experiences at Ambrose not only changed the way I work, but also how I live my life. First, I targeted my diet. I had heard about the benefits of a plant-based whole-foods diet. Skeptical at first, I warmed up to the idea after consulting with a vegetarian in the office. I will always remember the morning she dropped off samples of chia and ground flax seeds. (I mean, how else would I get my daily recommended Omega-3 fatty acids?!)

A few months later, I felt my energy levels increase, but the diet alone did not move the needle enough. Then came the Fitbit, a nifty little activity tracker that motivates me more than the drill sergeant from *Full Metal Jacket* ever could. Greg Slamowitz had one and talked about how it changed his daily habits, so I bought one.

I need only one hand on which to count how many days I've logged *less than* 10,000 steps since I acquired the Fitbit. Hooked from the start, a number of my colleagues and I created a group for Fitbit owners to leverage the power of community. At the time, there were maybe eight or nine of us, but we followed each other closely, praising one another for hitting new activity levels.

Soon thereafter, Ambrose as a company took a giant leap toward wellness by deciding to buy everyone a Fitbit. What an investment! Everyone in the company went wild. It's all we talked about in the office for weeks. Folks were going out for walking meetings. We started signing up for races (5K, 10K, half marathon). We switched out cereals in the kitchen for fresh fruit and oatmeal. The greatest impact of all came from sharing my personal goals with coworkers. We check in periodically and have a support system when self-control is vulnerable. For the first time, my ambitious wellness goals feel like they're within reach.

As someone who has struggled with work-life balance, it means a lot to work at a company that takes an interest in my personal well-being. I've never been a believer in a "clock in/ clock out" work environment. Too many people see work and life like oil and water. In fact, I think some of the best work that I've done is a result of ideas that came to me while on a long weekend walk. There's a great quote from Steven Johnson's book entitled *Where Good Ideas Come From: The Natural History of Innovation:*

> The history of innovation is replete with stories of good ideas that occurred to people while they were out on a stroll. The stroll removes you from the task-based focus of modern life—paying bills, answering e-mail, helping kids with homework—and deposits you in a more associative state. Given enough time, your mind will often stumble across some old connection that it had long overlooked, and you experience that delightful feeling of private serendipity: Why didn't I think of that before.

> Looking to develop a more productive and innovative workforce? Invest in your people's wellness. You will be amazed at the impact on the overall community.

WELLNESS METRICS

I do need to come back to metrics for a moment. If the proactive goal is to build a culture of wellness and to actually improve people's physical and mental wellbeing, you need metrics. You need all of your folks taking the Health Risk Assessment (HRA) on an annual or biannual basis. Their "family" members should also take the HRA.

Proper education and economic incentives are generally required to get solid participation, which I peg at over 80 percent. The HRA helps you to identify your company's physical and mental wellness issues, so you can put targeted programs in place that address these issues and then see if you can move the needle. Metrics are a critical component to a successful wellness program.

Another key component is a good understanding of behavioral economics. Successful wellness programs have built-in economics (rewards, prizes, premium rebates and discounts, and the like) that at first reward activities (walking more than 10,000 steps per day per month, for example) but then shift some economics toward specific outcomes such as targeted body mass index (BMI), good and bad cholesterol, blood sugar levels and so forth.

Our current Fitbit challenge has three main goals: health awareness, creating excitement, engagement and support around wellness, and increasing physical activity. So far, we are achieving these goals, but ultimately we need to measure whether this wellness initiative—and other such initiatives—actually improves general wellbeing.

Fortunately, based on the experience of larger companies, we know that wellness programs, when done correctly, have an incredibly positive return on investment, in addition to creating happy and healthy people.

CHAPTER SUMMARY

To fully activate the power of your organization you need a Constitutional Framework, a disciplined meeting rhythm, metric literacy, a strong, tribal culture and an organizational obsession with communicating. You also need the right players who embrace personal growth and engagement and build an organizational culture that supports physical and mental wellness and wellbeing. You want your team members to fully engage work and life. Mental and physical wellness needs to become a priority, as it is a proven strategy to winning on the individual company and national level.

Main chapter points include:

➢ Do you have the right people who embrace personal growth?

➤ A players attract A players; B players attract C players. You want to nurture A players who can turn B+ players into more A players!

➤ You must build a culture of wellness.

➤ Promote and support excellent mental health.

➤ Promote and support excellent physical health.

In the next chapter, I discuss the final, most essential ingredient for empowering the entire *Flip the Pyramid* methodology. It's passion—the fuel that unleashes the power and success of your people.

12

Find Your Passion, Period

To achieve success in your company transformation you need to find your passion. You also need others around you to do the same, and importantly, you need leadership within an organizational culture and framework that encourages and supports this endeavor.

This is how you move mountains. It is how you achieve big things.

When I first started to think about passion, I did so in a very personal and individualistic way. In Maslow's words, I needed to self-actualize. This is what made me feel great about myself. However, I often was frustrated in achieving this goal due to those around me, including the team or organization to which I belonged.

In fact, the more I learned about self-actualization, the more I realized that too often it is leadership and the organization, and its culture and structure, that inhibits individuals from reaching that goal. Professor McGregor wrote about this in his book *The Human Side of Enterprise.* So, as I thought more about the entire dynamic, I came to three conclusions: First, you need to find your passion and self-actualize—get to the top of Maslow's hierarchy of needs.

Second, you want everyone around you to do the same. Third, the first two will not occur unless you operate in an organizational culture and framework that encourages and supports passion and self-actualization in ways that align with one another and the organization.

If you are a leader, you have a responsibility to build an organization that encourages and supports the process. It took me years to figure this out.

This is strategic leadership. While it isn't easy, there is no doubt that you owe this experience to everyone who joins the organization. With the lessons of this book under your belt, I am confident that you will deliver on this responsibility.

If you are not in a position to help build an organization that encourages and supports aligned passion and self-actualization, then move on. Do not dither. Find a better place to work. Unfortunately, there are just too many organizations and leaders that want to hold people back, diminish them and throw cold water on their passion and enthusiasm. Do not waste your time with these places. You have a choice. Opt out now, look around, and instead find an encouraging, supportive culture—one seeking individuals who want to affirmatively opt in and passionately self-actualize. Hey, life is too short for anything less.

I started my passion quest with a very individual outlook, but once I traveled a bit down the road I realized that I was on to something a lot bigger than simply my own goals. For me, the passion became about building an organization that allowed others to actively participate, to make a difference, contribute, self-actualize and find their own passions. Once I came to this realization, and took the time and energy over several years to help transform Ambrose into this sort of company, my world radically changed. Now it is awesome to come to work where everyone is passionately aligned, engaged, empowered and on fire.

STEPPING BACK

In January 2011 I started to blog about my experiences in founding and growing Ambrose. Shortly after I started posting my thoughts, several Ambrose colleagues asked why I had left the socially and financially "comfortable" practice of law to cofound a startup.

It's a very good question. Why *did* I leave a "white shoe" law firm, where I earned a nice salary, to start a company where I ended up going 21 months without a paycheck? (I did not plan on going that long without a paycheck, and yes, it was rough.) The answer is simple: that is what I always wanted to do. But it did take me some time to figure that out.

Ever since I was a young boy I wanted to start and run a company (in grade school I had an imaginary company with my friend Mark Broydo). Why did I want to start a company since youth? Probably because that is what my father, my grandfather (Samuel Slamowitz) and my great grandfather (Isador Slamowitz) did for a living. They were all small business owners. Not by choice, but by default. There just were not many other options available for them.

My great grandfather was a shoemaker in Eastern Europe and then had a small shoe shop in Newark, New Jersey. My grandfather and great grandfather emigrated from Radom, Poland shortly after World Word I; the vast majority of their Jewish community that remained behind, approximately 32,000 people, were murdered by the Nazis 22 years later.

Isador Slamowitz, Newark, New Jersey (Peshine Avenue between Avon Avenue and Madison Avenue)

My grandfather started a very small food distribution company out of the trunk of his car in Newark during World War II, which my father eventually took over, and, years later, put into bankruptcy when I was a senior in high school and interest rates hit 21 percent. (Yes, his company was a borrower, and to this date, and because of this experience, I have an aversion to debt.) I grew up as a young boy "going to work" with my dad whenever I could; it was my favorite thing to do. Watching a business work is what I have always been passionate about since a young boy, and that is what matters: You must be passionate about what you do, period.

After all, if it weren't for that passion I would not have left a comfortable job to strike out for the unknown. I would not have stuck with Ambrose when the going got rough. I would not have explored what didn't work so well and take proactive steps to correct it. I would not have devoured management and organizational books by mentors such as Jim Collins, Douglas McGregor, Tony Hsieh, the Heath brothers, Clayton Christensen, Verne Harnish, Daniel Pink and others. And I would not have established the Constitutional Framework and amazing tribal culture we have at Ambrose today—the tribal culture that enables all of us to express ourselves, our passion and to self-actualize. While this journey started out as a personal one, that approach got me only so far. Eventually I was forced to learn that the journey is really about everyone else. The journey is about everyone around you as well. I wish I had learned this earlier.

A FALSE START

So why did I go to law school in the first place if I was so passionate about business back in the day? The truth is that I went for the wrong reason, as did many law students and lawyers, based on my conversations with them. I went because my mother told me to go to law school. Now many can and will power through law school (or medical school or whatever) because their mothers told them to, and honestly, I *did* love it, even though it was challenging. What I didn't realize, and what I do know now, is that you can't practice law for the rest of your life because your mother told you to. So while I loved law school, I derived no pleasure from the practice of law. Studying and practicing law are two very different beasts.

Practicing law was a horrible experience for me. I was a terrible lawyer and the reason for that was because I just wasn't passionate about it (not even close). The hours were long, the work was hard, and if you simply didn't have that passion, it became a very difficult undertaking.

I busted my butt in law school, worked hard and graduated near the top of my class, but I was very miserable when it came to practicing. It was a sobering and depressing experience. I was totally deflated. Many lawyers are unhappy with their career choice (they are practicing law for the wrong reasons: money and social and family prestige) so I then found myself working with unhappy people. How terrible is that? I spent several years assessing my situation and was at a loss.

The first law firm I worked for after graduation was a highly dysfunctional organization, but at that point, I couldn't tell whether it was me or them. Later I did join a more functional firm where I worked for a wonderfully supportive partner. It was at this point I realized that despite the organizational experience, the practice of law wasn't for me.

So success comes down to those three components: your passion, the passion of the people around you, and the culture and the framework of the organization in which you and your colleagues are allowed to self-actualize your passion. This is a necessary convergence.

FINDING PASSION IN *THE NEW YORK TIMES*

The New York Times obituary section was my savior. Since tenth grade, I had been an avid reader of that newspaper's in-depth obituaries. Some of my favorites are those written for Milton Petrie (1994), Paul Dean Arnold (1985), Ray Croc (1984), George Gallop (1984), Alfred Bloomingdale (1982), William Black (1983), Rudolph Schaefer (1982), Lila Wallace (1984), Alfred Knopf (1984), J. C. Hall (1982), J. W. Marriott (1985), Laura Ashley (1985), Herman Lay (1982), Max Stein (1982), Robert Woodruff (1984), Leon Hess (1999), Harry Helmsley (1997), Mark H. McCormack (2003) and Henry B. R. Brown (2008); I was lucky enough to know and spend some time with Mr. Brown while I was in high school.

Google these names and you will discover that they come with great personal stories about following your passion. I recall Mr. Brown, the inventor of the money market fund, telling me that the only reason he went to Harvard was because every male in his family had gone to Harvard since the 1700s and that he was very proud of the fact that he graduated near the bottom of his class! (I am sure he would love the fact that Mark Zuckerberg made it only through his first year.)

After reading the *New York Times* obituaries for years, I finally realized that the common thread was that all of these folks were passionate about what they did in life. So, while floundering with the practice of law, I took my cue from these obituaries and went to Plan B:

Find something that you really enjoy, something that you are passionate about.

For me, of course, that was founding and building a business.

PUTTING SOCIAL AND FAMILY PRESSURE ASIDE

There was a lot of social and family pressure on me to go to become a lawyer. These pressures, unfortunately, were working against self-actualization. When I left the practice of law in late 1996 for a startup, a fair number of people were shocked, even appalled, and thought I was foolish for leaving the practice of law. These forces were powerful but I just thought of all of those *New York Times* obituaries I had read.

Remember, this was before the entrepreneurial renaissance that came with the dot com boom. I recall several years after cofounding Ambrose, when refinancing my home mortgage with Citibank, I put down "entrepreneur" as my occupation and they told me that there is no such thing, and that I needed to change it to "small business owner." Wow, isn't that diminishing? In fact, in the mid-to late-1990s, in New York City there was still a social stigma around entrepreneurship. Socially we have come a very long way (for example, Mark Zuckerberg as *Time Magazine's* "Person of the Year" in 2010).

Moral of the story: Regardless of family and social pressures, have the fortitude to buck any such diminishing pressures and follow your passion. My advice to young people who come to me for career advice is that they need to put those social and family pressures aside. Put them in a box, close it up, and place it somewhere far away. Find your passion, surround yourself with other people who have found their passion, and find an organization that supports and encourages your passion and the passion of those around you. Again, you need all three.

FOCUSING YOUR PASSION ON ORGANIZATIONAL TRANSFORMATION

I left the practice of law, cofounded Ambrose and felt great—for a while, anyway. Then something happened: success.

Today I spend a lot of time travelling around the country speaking with entrepreneurs. It is awesome to speak with people who are following their dream, self-actualizing, finding their passion. While I enthusiastically encourage all of these people, I warn them: Be careful, success happens. Brute force, micromanagement and individual heroics will get you only so far. As I have described, it only got us so far, and then we hit a wall and we were simply stuck in the mud. I began to dislike my "job" as an entrepreneur.

I tell entrepreneurs and organizational leaders that they must quickly realize that it isn't just about them. It isn't only about their passion and their right to self-actualize, but is also about everyone else's passion and right to self actualize, so start to build an organizational culture and framework now that will help to make this happen. This is how you build a truly great organization that will achieve big things.

YOU CAN DO IT

As a leader, you must quickly move past your own ego and individual heroics, and realize that with leadership comes a responsibility to build an organization that supports and encourages organization-wide self-actualization. It isn't about you. It is about everyone else around you. I recently told a group of entrepreneurs in Hoboken, New Jersey, that you want your receptionist feeling great every single day and firing on all pistons. That is your job as a leader.

It isn't easy, but we are doing it. It has taken a lot of learning, a lot of trial and error and time. It doesn't happen overnight. It took us a solid three years to go through this transformation, but we did start very late in our organizational life cycle. It is for this reason that I encourage entrepreneurs and startup organizations to build an organization that supports and encourages self-actualization from the beginning. This is a never-ending journey and something that I constantly worry about. As a leader, this is what keeps me up at night.

If you are a leader, start building the organizational construct that will empower every single person in your organization to find his or her passion and to self-actualize. Build an incredibly strong Constitutional Framework: core values, BHAG, annual and quarterly goals, brand promise and core purpose. Put in place a disciplined meeting rhythm. Teach metrics literacy. Create a strong, tribal culture, and instill an obsession with communication.

You also need a deeply ingrained organizational comfort with change, risk, failure, experimentation, learning and constant improvement. You then need to attract awesome human capital into this construct, coach them, support excellent physical and mental well being and enable everyone to passionately self-actualize—to the point of expecting this. Within this organizational framework, liberate your organization's human capital. Magic will happen.

Command, control and micromanagement at first appear to be the easy road, but do not be tempted by this route. It leads to misery for all involved. The road first clearly articulated by Professors McGregor and Maslow at first appears the harder road. In the end, it is not.

You don't have to go down this road alone. There is a lot written and many other leaders and organizations who have already taken the journey.

I hope our story, and this book, teaches and encourages you to take the less travelled road first staked out by McGregor and Maslow. Fifty years later, it is now a well-marked route. It is also a fun and rewarding experience to build and participate in an organization where everyone is passionately self-actualizing.

You can do this, and it will give you an incredibly competitive advantage. So build or join an organization where everyone participates in the journey, where everyone is aligned, engaged, empowered and on fire. Do not dither. Do not dally. Start today, and have an awesome journey.

Appendix

Greg's Reading List

These books and articles have taught me a lot about business, people and life. They are listed in no particular order. Enjoy.

- *Multipliers: How the Best Leaders Make Everyone Smarter* by Liz Wiseman and Greg McKeown
- *Switch: How to Change Things When Change Is Hard* by Chip and Dan Heath
- *Tribal Leadership* by Dave Logan, John King and Halee Fischer-Wright
- *Employees First, Customers Second* by Vineet Nayar
- *Carrots and Sticks Don't Work* by Dr. Paul Marciano
- *Leading Change* by John Kotter
- *Buy-In* by John Kotter
- *Delivering Happiness: A Path to Profits, Passion, and Purpose* by Tony Hsieh
- *Start-Up Nation: The Story of Israel's Economic Miracle* by Dan Senor and Soul Singer
- *What Would Google Do?* by Jeff Jarvis

- *Death By Meeting* by Patrick Lencioni
- *The Five Dysfunctions of a Team* by Patrick Lencioni
- *Blue Ocean Strategy* by W. Chan Kim and Renee Mauborgne (article from Harvard Business Review; reprint R0410D, October 2004)
- *Building Your Company's Vision* by James C. Collins and Jerry I. Porras (article from Harvard Business Review; reprint 96501, Sept–Oct 1996)
- *Tribes: We Need You to Lead Us* by Seth Godin
- *Good to Great* by Jim Collins
- *Great by Choice* by Jim Collins
- *Hidden Champions of the 21st Century* by Hermann Simon
- *The Inside Advantage* by Robert H. Bloom
- *DRiVE* by Daniel Pink
- *A Whole New Mind: Why Right-Brainers Will Rule the Future* by Daniel Pink
- *MoneyBall!* by Michael Lewis
- *Leadership the Hard Way* by Dov Frohman and Robert Howard
- *Raving Fans* by Ken Blanchard
- *The Little Engine That Could* by Watty Piper
- *The No Asshole Rule* by Prof. Robert Sutton
- *Goldman Sach's The Culture of Success* by Lisa Endlich
- *The Ultimate Question* by Fred Reichheld
- *Emotional Intelligence 2.0* by Travis Bradberry, Jean Greaves and Patrick M. Lencioni
- *Different: Escaping the Competitive Herd* by Youngme Moon
- *Leading with the Heart: Coach K's Successful Strategies for Basketball, Business, and Life* by Mike Krzyzewski and Donald T. Phillips

- ➤ *What Got You Here Won't Get You There: How Successful People Become Even More Successful* by Marshall Goldsmith and Mark Reiter

- ➤ *Linchpin: Are You Indispensable?* by Seth Godin

- ➤ *Titan: The Life of John D. Rockefeller, Sr.* by Ron Chernow

- ➤ *The Great Game of Business* by Jack Stack and Bo Burlingham

- ➤ *Douglas McGregor, Revisited: Managing the Human Side of the Enterprise* by Gary Heil, Warren Bennis and Deborah C. Stephens

- ➤ *How Will You Measure Your Life?* by Clayton M. Christensen, James Allworth and Karen Dillon

- ➤ *Innovator's Dilemma: The Revolutionary Book That Will Change the Way You Do Business* by Clayton M. Christensen

- ➤ *Turn the Ship Around: How to Create Leadership at Every Level* by L. David Marquet, Captain U.S. Navy (Retired)

- ➤ *SPIN Selling* by Neil Rackham

- ➤ *The Ultimate Sales Machine* by Chet Holmes

- ➤ *The Inside Advantage* and *The New Experts,* both by Robert H. Bloom

- ➤ *Inbound Marketing* by Brian Halligan, Dharmesh Shah and David Meerman Scott

- ➤ *Real-Time Marketing and PR* by David Meerman Scott

- ➤ *All Marketers Are Liars Tell Stories* by Seth Godin

- ➤ *Reality Marketing Revolution* by Eric Keiles and Mike Lieberman

- ➤ *Different: Escaping the Competitive Herd* and other titles by Youngme Moon

About the Author

Greg Slamowitz is Founder and Chairman of the Board of WellnessRebates LLC (**www.wellnessrebates.com**), a wellness solutions designer and administrator for mid-size and large employers. He is also a Cofounder and Co-CEO of Ambrose Employer Group, LLC (**www.ambrose.com**), a professional employer organization (PEO), which recently ranked among Crain's New York's list of the 50 fastest growing companies. For the past two consecutive years Ambrose also has been recognized by the New York State Society for Human Resource Management as one of the "Best Companies to Work For in New York." Greg enjoys learning and teaching and has spent considerable time over the last several years meeting with entrepreneurs and business leaders. He regularly presents his seminar, "Flip the Pyramid," around the United States.

Greg also has spent significant time in Washington DC with members and staffers of the U.S. Senate and House of Representatives, whom he has briefed on the challenges to and solutions for small and mid-sized businesses. Greg is passionate about helping America's businesses focus on growth, profit, hiring and creating an awesome and healthy experience for each and every working American.

Prior to cofounding Ambrose in 1997, Greg practiced tax law with Brown & Wood (now Sidley Austin Brown & Wood) in New York City. He holds two law degrees—a Master of Laws in Taxation from New York University School of Law, and a Juris Doctorate, with distinction, from Emory University School of Law in Atlanta. He received his undergraduate degree, cum laude, from New York University.

Greg was the recipient of the 2001 Ernst & Young New York Entrepreneur of the Year® award in the employment services category. Greg also serves on the Dean's Advisory Board for Emory University's School of Law.

Please visit Greg's personal blog at **www.gregslamowitz.com**, his LinkedIn Profile at **http://www.linkedin.com/pub/greg-slamowitz/5/814/176** and Twitter **@gregslamowitz**.

Greg's passions include developing highly functional organizations, engaged cultures, health care and wellness, skiing and sailing (**www.teammanitou.com**).

Index

Colophon

Publisher/Editorial Director: Michael Roney

Art Director: Sarah M. Clarehart

Copyeditor/Proofreader: Michael D. Welch

Indexer: Melody Englund

Contact: info@highpointpubs.com